A PROFESSOR
IN DISGUISE

A PROFESSOR IN DISGUISE

FEY RABINDRON

A PROFESSOR IN DISGUISE

iUniverse books may be ordered through booksellers or by contacting:

iUniverse
1663 Liberty Drive
Bloomington, IN 47403
www.iuniverse.com
1-800-Authors (1-800-288-4677)

Because of the dynamic nature of the Internet, any web addresses or links contained in this book may have changed since publication and may no longer be valid. The views expressed in this work are solely those of the author and do not necessarily reflect the views of the publisher, and the publisher hereby disclaims any responsibility for them.

Any people depicted in stock imagery provided by Getty Images are models, and such images are being used for illustrative purposes only. Certain stock imagery © Getty Images.

ISBN: 978-1-5320-5479-2 (sc)
ISBN: 978-1-5320-5480-8 (e)

Library of Congress Control Number: 2018908857

Print information available on the last page.

iUniverse rev. date: 07/30/2018

INTRODUCTION

It is a long time now since I have decided to write the story of my life. I have become a full professor at my Hometown University, but when I think about my life and go through my memories, I think that I have really been a fool throughout my life. The respectable position that I have earned in our society, is due to location and time I think. I admit that I have had enough perseverance in my life to become successful in work and earning a respectable life, however, in married life, I have not been successful. I hope you not only enjoy reading this book, but that you learn something from reading it too. Here is the first volume of the book. It is divided into five chapters. Chapter 1 concerns the temptations regarding writing the book. Chapter 2 is about my childhood and my school studies. Chapter 3 is about my studies in England. Chapter 4 is about my first marriage and chapter five about my second one. I have changed the names of persons involved in the story as far as I could. I want the persons and the locations to be anonymous.

CHAPTER 1

Temptations for writing the book

It was winter of nineteen years ago (1999). My father was ill and had to have an operation for his prostate. My sister and her husband who is also my cousin and a gynaecologist insisted that I go with my father to The Capital accompanying my father. It was in the middle of term and I was reluctant to interrupt my lectures with the students. However, I decided to go. My daughter had moved to The Capital not long time ago and was living with her in-laws, so I liked very much to go and see where she was living and how she was spending her life with two children in her in-law's house. Air tickets were bought for us that are for my father, mother, my sister and me. My father was holding his urine glass in his hands and carrying it with him in the airport! He wanted to show to the people that he was really ill and unhappy. He believed in the influence by evil eye, he was rather superstitious. The airport attendance came to him and said you cannot carry this glass of urine with you like this; you must hide it inside your shirt. Therefore, he obeyed him and we embarked on the plane safely. After an hour, we arrived in The Capital Airport and went to my sister's apartment with a taxi. It was rather cold but the apartment was cosy and warm. The next morning my father was taken to the hospital, where my cousin had made all arrangements for his operation. I accompanied him while my mother and sister stayed at home. He was supposed to be there for three days. The first day was for making necessary medical tests and obtaining lab reports. I stayed there all the day. My sister came in the evening and told me that I could go to my daughter's house and stay the night with her and return to the hospital next morning when my father would be taken to the operation room.

I arrived in my daughter's house in the evening. She had made dinner for me. Her children, a two years old daughter and a three months old son went to sleep soon and we were alone. My daughter's husband worked in a nearby city and would not come until weekend. It was about 10 p.m. that she sat next to me and we started talking. It was the first time that I had obtained the opportunity to talk to her freely without any apprehension. She said:

- Dad: you did not marry your English girlfriend while you were studying in England, why was that?
- Why do you ask this question?
- If you had married her, I would have been born in England, I would have been an English girl and probably would have enjoyed my life much more than the life I have had in my country.
- Even if I had married her, I would have returned home after my studies and most probably, I would have divorced her, so you had to grow up without your mother!
- You married another girl and I hear that your marriage broke up, why was that?
- It is a long story, probably I cannot tell you all that happened, and I am ashamed to tell you some of the events.
- It must be very interesting dad, why you do not write your memories. I say, it must be interesting!
- You are right, I have thought about it and I must write a book telling the story of my life.
- Yes, dad, do that do that, I encourage you to write down your memories; it would be at least interesting for me.

After this conversation, I decided to put down my memories, but I have been lazy to sit down, think and write it up. It is now fifteen years since I made up my mind to write a book. I was retired ten years ago and my first decision was to write a book about my life. I had decided to write it in English, because I cannot express some of the events freely in my own language. However, I did not aspire to start; there was always something there to put me off from writing. Now that I have finally decided to write my memories, I think I should start from my childhood and proceed from then on.

Concluding remark: I have always postponed things I had to do to a later time. I must be a lazy person somehow.

CHAPTER 2

1-2 My Childhood

I was born just after the Second World War had finished in a deserted town in my country. At birth, my father was 27 years old and my mother was about 14 years old. They were cousins and the family was looked at as a reasonably well off concerning the society and the economic situation of those days. The Second World War had just finished but the aftermath of the war was affecting the economic situation. A year later, my mother gave birth to another child. My eldest sister was born. In the following year another sister was born. She was poisoned by out-dated dried milk when she was only 6 months old and she passed away soon. A couple of years later, my mother gave birth to a son. My father respected him very much. I remember him vaguely. I was sent to the school at the age of six in 1951. I never forget the first day I was sent to the school. Neither my father nor my mother took me to the school. The son of our gardener took me to the school with his bicycle. I even did not know where I was going. On the way he told me that he is taking me to school, he said it is a nice place. When we got there, he wanted to leave me there and go home. It was a strange place for me and I started crying as most children do on their first day of schooling. Therefore, he stayed there in front of the classroom such that I could see him. After a while, the teacher, who was a nice and pleasant woman, talked to me and apparently had pointed at him to leave. When I noticed that he had vanished, I cried again but the teacher kindly told me not to cry and said you are not alone. You can find some friends here and can play with them later.

A couple of months later, sometime in autumn, on my return from school I heard lots of screaming coming out from our house. My brother was drowned in the pool! My mother had become short of hearing. There was a deaf woman helping her cleaning vegetables next to the pool. My brother was playing around and had gone to play with water in the pool. He had fallen into the pool quietly; they had noticed a body on the surface of the pool when it was too late to do anything. It was a terrible experience for me. The year before that my grandmother had died and I vaguely remember my uncle screaming wanting to kill himself by a knife! My uncle died from a car accident some years later. Now the situation was much worse. My father was also very upset but he convinced himself that God had given him and God had taken him, it was because he had been too proud of himself and unthankful. In winter, I had gone to one of my schoolmate's house on the way back home. He insisted me to stay with him and I was busy playing. I was only seven years old; an innocent child, suddenly I realized that I had stayed there for a long time, so I rushed home. My parents were waiting for my arrival from school. They had been looking for me everywhere, had gone to the school and had asked people going by if they had seen a child. They were very worried especially since they had lost their son few months before that. On my arrival, my father asked me where I had been. I said I was in my friend's house (who was my mother's relative and our neighbour). My father took my arms and pushed me to a small dark room we used to use as a store. It was dark and I was very frightened from the darkness and the possibility of all kinds of insects being there like beetles and scorpion. I was there probably for 10 minutes before my mother came and mediated for me. From then on, I was very afraid of my father. Pushing me into a dark and cold store in the middle of winter affected roots of my soul and my mind. I must admit that I was potentially shy but I think this event made me frightened of playing freely with my schoolmates. Even then I always respected him very much and was very sad when he died some years later from diabetes, a disease very common in my hometown. A year later my second sister was born. She was very dear to my parents because she was born after the death of their two children. The years in elementary school passed quickly. I do not have glittering memories from those days. Nothing extraordinary happened. Two years later, my mother gave birth to my third sister. My mother got ill on her birth and was very unhappy about it for many years. In those years, we had a servant and a maidservant as well. I think there is no point bringing out memories regarding the events happening in the house although some of them had influenced me and probably affected my future carrier. In the school I was ranked as a rather sharp student; I was among the first top five students in the class. They were more than thirty students in the classroom. I do not remember exactly how many students were in the classes. All I remember is that I was always encouraged by my teachers also by my father and this encouragement pursued me to study and try to be a top student. When I was in the sixth year of school and was only twelve years old, I was amazed to hear some rude and dirty words between my classmates. My parents never used dirty vocabulary at home. However, these students not only used four letter words for sexual relation, but also pretended acting it in their conversation and also tried to show off that they knew a lot about this taboo vocabulary in our society. Mind you talking to girls or women was very restricted, we only could hear our own family's female voice or maidservants. On the way to school we could see girls going to school or coming out of school (in fact my sister's school was very close to my school and we used to walk together our way from home to school) but never dared to look at them never mind talking to them. My schoolmates always talked about being with a handsome boy and overstated that they had a friend with nice buttocks or that they had very intimate relation with him! One day, after the exam, which was held early in the morning, we were told to go home, but many of us did not go home. We went to a playground playing football. We had a schoolmate who was from The Capital. He had a posh accent and was very handsome. We had also a schoolmate who was very rude and perhaps one or two years older than he was. Suddenly he took the handsome boy in his arms from behind and pretended as if he was having intimate relation with him. Poor boy was screaming and trying to get out of his arms. Although no trousers were taken off or nothing rude had happened but the next day the rumours spread that the rude boy had sexual relation with the handsome boy outside the school in front of his classmates! This event triggered something happening into my mind. Slang vocabulary for boys and girl's sexual parts were new to me. I enjoyed hearing them and I repeated these words when I was alone. Later I was experiencing erection. No one in the family nor the teachers or classmates explained what was happening to my classmates or me. I was being matured without knowing what it meant! In the following spring, one of my aunts had come to our town from where she lived to visit us. She had brought his six-year-old son with her. One afternoon I took him on my bike for a ride in the deserted and isolated back streets near our home. I held him in my arms from behind as the rude boy had held the handsome boy. I enjoyed myself a lot. Poor boy did not say anything, perhaps he did not know what it meant. I also did not know what exactly sexual relation was. This was my first real experience in that age. I thought I had become a man and was feeling proud of myself. Years after whenever I saw this cousin of mine, I always remembered that event and wanted to know if he remembered it too. I never dared to ask him but probably he must have remembered something about it. By the way, my mother had given birth to twin boys. Actually, one of them was half an hour older than the other one. Later when they had grown up the elder one always reminded him that he was older and expected him to respect him! This sounded funny to me! Now my mother was very busy, had six children to care about and so she never had time to ask my elder sister or me about our daily life. As far as we were going to our schools regularly and were not ill, she was happy. My father had his own problems. Making money for a big family was not a simple thing. Besides, the new-born children amused my parents a lot. So they never showed worried about their other children.

In winter of following year, one night I was dreaming about that handsome schoolmate. Dreaming that I was holding him in my arms like the rude boy had done and that I was holding him tight. Early in the morning, while was thinking about this strange dream I suddenly wetted myself. It was a very enjoyable experience. Later that day I thought, I had harmed myself and I was very worried. I did not dare to tell my experience to anybody even to my schoolmates. In the night when we slept, I tried to review the last night's event. To my delight, I noticed that as I was remembering my dream I was getting excited again; this time even more than the night before. I was not worried any more. Soon after, I had wetted my pyjamas. I got worried about this wetness! If my mother asked me in the morning, what should I say? Now I had discovered these kinds of dreams bring a lot of delight and that nothing wrong had happened to me!

Remarks: sexual relation was taboo in those days; we never talked about it and knew nothing about it as well. Parents expected their children to learn about it from their schoolmates or friends of the same age, or relatives of the same age! Self-abusing was a phenomenon in most families, worse than that homosexuality was wide spread especially in rural places.

2-2 Life in the fifties in my birthplace

I remember life in my birthplace vaguely before I went to school. The electricity was limited, from sunset, say, 5 p.m. in autumn and winter, up to 11 p.m. I think full electricity did establish in 1956. In addition, there were few cars in the streets, apparently taxi service started from 1952. There was no bus service inside the town, only in between cities or villages. There were plenty of cyclists and my first bicycle was bought for me in 1955. I was afraid riding it and I remember two of my classmates came to our house and taught me how to ride a bicycle. It took me about a week to learn riding my bicycle. I used to go to school with my bike from then on until I left my hometown. My elder sister, used to walk to school accompanied by a servant. He was a Negro whose parents were brought to my country during the era when buying slaves was a usual practice. In fact, he was my grandfather's slave and he had sent him to work for us as a servant. Slavery had been demolished during twentieth century, but he considered himself a faithful servant rather than a slave. He was a very good cook for us, used to do all the shopping and cooking for us and besides accompanied my sister to the school at least twice a day. He came to stay with us during fifties and stayed with us for ten years. The story why he left is quite interesting; I will come to that later. Buses had front boots and roared like monsters while going up hills. Cooking was with wood; oil burning cookers or heaters were not in the markets yet. In winter, we used to warm the rooms by coals brought into glow in brazier in fresh air and then taken into the rooms. Actually, life was rather primitive. Few people had radios. In 1953, my father bought an electric Philips radio. It was quite big and took about a minute to warm up. I remember one afternoon when it was reading the news bulletin, my sister and I insisted to look into back of the radio and search for small iron men sitting inside the radio! Travelling those days was very hard I remember. We used to go to a holy city far from my hometown every summer after school break in summer; it usually began first day of June. There were two garages in The Big City centre; the one we used to travel with was nearer to our house. The respectable people would insist to sit in front and they used to come after other people. The bus assistant used to take about one hour to make the passengers seated, because they had sold the same seat number to several people! If the bus was supposed to leave at 2 p.m. it would leave at 4 p.m. and that was why respected people arrived rather late, sometimes they had to phone them (if they were on the phone) or send someone to inform them that the bus was ready to go! After returning from the holy city, we used to go to a nearby village, where we had a big garden there, and its climate was very mild and pleasant in midst of summer heat.

During fifties, most people were very fanatic. In our city, all women used to wear hijab, and hardly appeared in the streets without a male company; this could have been their son, brother or husband. The women were very careful about their hijab and were fully covered. You could only see their face. Talking with girls or women other than close relatives was taboo. So hearing voice of a stranger woman could be very exciting. I remember when I was about 16 years old; a widowed woman rented our neighbouring house. She had a young girl whom I never saw, probably aged sixteen or seventeen. In the evenings when I was studying in my room, I could hear her singing, then I used to concentrate on hearing her voice, which was penetrating through the wall between our rooms, and I enjoyed a lot listening to a female stranger voice. My sister used to go to school with our servant accompanying her. The girl's schools usually started at least a quarter of an hour sooner and finished a quarter of an hour later than boy's schools; all planned so that boys would not intrude girls on their way home. As a result, homosexuality between men was very common. I do not know much about homosexuality between women, but I am sure that must have been a common practice as well. I remember once when I was returning home on my bike from the school, a man approached me and told me for whom do you want to keep it? Let us enjoy ourselves!

Of course, he had made a pass on me and wanted to have intimate relation! I was too young to understand his purpose; but now, after so many years, I think how dirty minded were men in our society.

There were no bathrooms in the houses. The water and heating was the main problem. In our house (and most houses of well-off families), there was a deep well, probably forty meters or more deep. There was a reservoir next to it and a man used to come two or three times a week and draw water from the well by bucket for up to 2 or 3 hours. These men were very poor, but even then were happy to have a job. They were not paid much for the hard work they did. This water from the well was used for drinking, cooking and washing. It turned out rather expensive. For heating, we did not have oil heaters or even oil cookers. They were brought to our city in winter of 1956 as I remember. Therefore, before that we used firewood for cooking and coal for heating. We used to go to public bath once a week, usually on Thursdays. Up to age of ten, I used to go with my mother and sisters. We would sit and wait in the waiting hall until a private bath was ready to use. Then we would go inside and take our cloths off. All of us would be naked! After a few minutes, a female rubber or a masseur would come in and would massage us harshly and wash us with soap and white powder until really cleaned. Of course, this woman rubber would take her clothes off and when in the bath room all were naked. I remember when I was ten years old I was staring at between her legs while she was rubbing my head with soap, she then told my mother that this boy is old enough now and you should send him to bath with his father. The next time I went to public bath with my father; the male rubber cleansed my father first and then he started rubbing and washing me. I remember that I had a look on good-looking boys in the classroom. In my hometown in the fifties, most boys had boyfriends, and especially those who were well off would go out with handsome boys and spend money for them. There was a handsome boy in our class when I was at high school. He was from a poor family sent over to our city to study in high school. He had rented a house with his cousins and was living in poor conditions. I was from a well off family and I used to spend a lot of money on him. For instance, if we went to barber together, I would pay for both of us. I used to invite him to have ice cream or soft drinks together. Later I had invited private teachers to come to our house to work mathematics, English and physics with me. I had asked my schoolmate to come to our house and benefit from private tuition. When the teacher would leave, I used to get myself very close to him and put my hands on his thigh and this gave me a lot of enjoyment. I am sure he knew about my dirty feelings but that was an accepted behaviour. He never declined me, however, I never dared to go further and tell him that I wanted to hold him in my arms. I am telling this to explain that since there was no communication with outside girls or women and even harsh contacts with boys regarding sexual instinct, so most boys and I abused ourselves. However, some could control themselves, but I could not. I started abusing myself from the age of thirteen, just in the beginning of adultness. Soon it affected my eyes and I was short sighted from the age of fourteen. I visited an optician on my own and he prescribed a lens for me but my parents thought I wanted to wear glasses for showing off. Three years later, I could not read the blackboard even from the front row. This time the optician told me why I had not used glasses before and said if you do not wear glasses, soon you would go blind. I bought a pair of glasses with the prescribed lens and it took me about a month to get used to wearing glasses. I was only sixteen years old and I did not know what had affected my eyes. This self-abusing, gradually made me isolated from the society as well. I did not have many friends. Only I had the handsome schoolmate and another friend who was competent with me. In summers, we used to go to the village, and stay there for about three months. When I was sixteen years old, I went out a lot with a boy who was a relative. He was slim and nice looking boy, only one year younger than I was. When we walked alone along narrow streets of the village, which usually was deserted and very quiet, or at least at the hours when there was nobody present (early evenings)

I used to get myself very close to him. Sometimes I fingered him very gently; he surely did feel my fingers, but never refused or said anything. I think he probably enjoyed it too, but I never dared to go further and say anything to him. This fingering was very exciting and when back home I used to imagine him and me in the garden under the trees lying next to each other and you know what.

Now when I think about those memories, I get sorry for myself. I not only was a simple boy but also a fool as well. I think some women also masturbated or had lesbian inclinations. I remember one summer in the village; I was coming out from the toilets when I heard a sound coming from a deserted kitchen. I got myself closer to the kitchen and I heard as if a woman was excited from having sex. I got closer, I saw this woman who had come to milk one of my twin brothers. She had left her baby besides herself, apparently was fast asleep. She was sitting on her feet bending over and abusing her self. I got closer and somewhat tried to enjoy myself but she noticed me and screamed what do you want and what are you looking at? I ran away. She was short sighted as well and now I am sure it was because she used to abuse herself a lot. About ten years later I heard that she died from diabetes although she was rather young, probably in her early forties. This shows that some women either masturbated like men or had homosexual feelings as men had. The strict rules keeping men and women away from each other, which was governing the religious communities, had caused natural contacts as in Western countries to be very limited.

There was a place in our city for prostitutes. I heard about it when I was fifteen. In fact, it was near the garden house in which we used to move during spring and live until end of summer time. When I was sixteen years old, one afternoon about two o'clock, I decided to go to this place. Actually, I had visited this place with some schoolmates some months before, cycling through it. The houses were situated in a narrow road about sixty meters long. Both sides were some old brick made houses, probably ten houses altogether. The doors were open and some women with their hijabs were sitting on front door, showing a bit of their hair as men passed by. Some were young, slim heavily powdered, and had a makeup on their face, while others were very plain. As I was driving my bicycle with my schoolmates, I tried to stare at these women. I was embarrassed a bit. I remember one of the schoolmates cried out it is only twenty-five cents (regarding the dollar value at those days), let us pay and enjoy ourselves! I always pretended that I was a very smart boy and this was a sin and would not do it. While inside me there was a storm, immediately, I planned to come and visit this place on my own, sometime that no one would see me! Any way that autumn afternoon arrived. A young girl in her twenties was sitting outside a house. As I passed away, she smiled at me and sort of invited me with her eyes following me. I was very excited and very embarrassed as well. I did not know what to do and what to say, so I accelerated and got away from her. Some five minutes later, I decided to come back and talk to her, but on my return, she had disappeared. I guess, she had found a customer. A few houses onwards, I saw a woman in her forties sitting. This time she called me and said do not be shy I am here for you. I stopped and parked my bike at the corner of her house. She soon took me inside, got naked and told me to get on with it! I stared at her for a while; she was rather fat and ugly. She did not use a preservative, perhaps there were no preservatives in the market yet. At least I had not heard about it at all. As soon as I penetrated her, I had orgasm. It took me about ten seconds I think. She cleaned herself with some cotton and asked me if I enjoyed it. I paid her (about 25 cents) and left her house quickly. I was worried if someone had seen me. More I was regretting why I had not stopped in front of that young woman, how unfortunate I was. It was my own fault, I was very shy and if this elder woman had not invited me probably, I would have run away from her as well. This was my first experience having sex relation with a real woman. The girl I had seen few minutes before this one was young and beautiful. Anyway, I was not satisfied with my first experience, as I had expected.

Two years later, I was in The Capital in summer time in my grandfather's house. I had gone to The Capital to go to English language school. They had a chauffeur who lived with his family in their house. The chauffeur had a son who was two years younger than I was. He was fifteen years old and had a handsome look. He did not like studying and her mother wanted me to stay with him and persuade him to study. He had failed some lessons and was preparing for a reset exam at the end of summer. The chauffeur expected me to work with his son and I thought it was a good thing for me. He was very naughty and did not like studying at all. One day he had invited one of his schoolmates to stay the night with him. That night we slept on the terrace of the house. Later I noticed that he was very intimate with his schoolmate and actually had sexual relation with him. A few days later, the son of chauffeur said to his mother he was going to cinema with his friends however, he did not invite me to go with them. I was shy and did not complain. When returned home, he said they had gone to a suburb in The Capital where prostitutes where kept in. He said they had enjoyed themselves very much, and each had visited two or three different sluts. A few days later, he went out again with his father, pretending he was going to study with one of his schoolmates. Two weeks later, he was going out every day visiting a doctor! He was infected a disease from one of those sluts, because they did not use any protective. When I heard this, I was so glad that I had not gone with them. However, I wished to go to that suburb one day on my own and visit the place. This happened some four or five years later. I was staying in my grandfather's house. One evening I got a taxi and went to this place. I paid one dollar for a slut. The woman was rather nice looking. It was a quick experience as usual. Later I was walking along the place. At some houses, I could hear someone playing music, I peered through, I could see a girl dancing while four or five men were clapping their hands and watching her dance. This woman was amusing the men while there was another woman giving her service to the customers. These men were in a queue waiting for their turn. The place was full of men addicted to opium or perhaps other things like heroin. About half an hour later, I visited another woman. I paid her one dollar as well, but this time it took me longer. The poor woman worked on me hard to make me excited! I did not enjoy myself as I did with the first slut!

Remarks: From 1950 to 1955, life was very simple. As from 1955 to 1960, rapid improvement in technology affected our lives. Oil heaters, fans, transistor radios, ice cream and soft drinks influenced our daily life. Compared with nowadays, it appears that we jumped forward suddenly for 50 years! It appears as if life in my hometown during the years 1950-1955, was the same as life in medieval period of my country. As a teenager, I was sexually depressed and frustrated with self-abusing. I had one or two unsuccessful experience with sluts, but depression had made me isolated, dissociable, shy and frustrated.

3-2 My studies in my hometown

I went to elementary school in early fifties. I do not remember much from my first year in the school except the first day and going to my schoolmate's house which I have explained before. We had a woman teacher who was very kind. One day in dictation, I missed a vowel and she gave me 19.5 out of twenty. I cried a lot, so much that she changed it to twenty. I was afraid of my father to punish me. The second year I registered at a different school. I studied there for five years until I got my elementary school certificate. I was rather shy and did not have many friends. I did my homeworks on time. I was not very clever, only studied hard. My father used to help me in mathematics but when I got older, my father never bothered to teach me maths any more. He sometimes worked English alphabet or simple words and my own language literature, but that was all. I finished elementary school with an overall average of 16.5 out of 20. I was ranked among the first top five students of the school. After finishing the school, I went to a famous high school to register. It was a well-known high school in our time; it was well known for its good and experienced teachers. Of course, my father did not come with me for registration. To my surprise, they told me they would not register students coming from elementary schools anymore and told me to go and register in a newly made High School. Well I did not have another choice, the term had started and there was no one to give me advice as where to register. Of course, there were three other well-known high schools in our town but I thought that was my fate, and I registered at this newly built High School. I studied there for another three years. In the class, soon I noticed that I could not read the blackboard when seated at the rare of the classroom. I moved to the front. I was sure I was short sighted. I went to an optician on my own. My parents did not accompany me. He gave me a prescription and told me to wear glasses. I do not know why my parents especially my father did not approve the optician and did not buy glasses for me. Perhaps it was my own fault because I did not insist. Year after year, my eyesight got worse until when I was 16, I noticed that I could not read the blackboard even when seated in the front row. I have an unforgettable memory from this high school. It was in the third year (final year). The headmaster had arranged a competition among three top students of the class. It was held in an evening. The competition was held in a classroom with all teachers and the head master present. We had to guess what they had written on a piece of paper within 20 questions. If we could guess right, we would win. The other two contestants could not guess it right. It was my turn. I got very close to the answer. The room was quiet, everybody was staring at me, some tried to tell me the question by whispering or other kinds of figuring; but I could not figure out their suggestions. Suddenly I thought, as I was very interested in electricity, (in fact in the second year, I had taken an instrument to the physics laboratory for water decomposition; this was made of a glass vessel, which had two small holes at the bottom. I had passed two gold wires through them and ceiled it with red glue made for stamps. I was admired for that by my teachers and schoolmates as well) and as I had suggested nearly all electric instruments, the only thing I had not suggested was the doorbell. It was my last opportunity to guess the answer; I had 30 seconds left! I then shouted is it the doorbell? All the students and the teachers hoorayed and clapped their hands for me. The headmaster signed the front page of a book of poems and gave it to me. This contest showed that although I was rather slow in progress but I could manage getting out of the problem after hard thinking!

After three years studying, I registered in a famous High School. I had chosen to read mathematics as my major subjects. At those days, students had three choices: mathematics whose graduates from the high school would attempt for engineering subjects at university; biology whose graduates would attempt for medical science and finally literature whose graduates would attempt related subjects like history, geography and of course literature. This high school was very popular in our city and very populated. We were divided in two classrooms, (a) and (b). I do not remember which class I was in, but as I was known as a hard working student and very clever among the students, all students of the high school knew me. I only remember a few classmates after so many years. Even then, I knew only few of my classmates. In the first year, I met a handsome boy whom I have mentioned him before and became very friendly with him. He was quite handsome and many other students wanted to be friends with him. However, later he was known as my boyfriend and perhaps other schoolmates never made a pass on him at least in front of me. I tried to be with him as much as I could. I sat next to him in the classroom, I asked him to come to our house for private tuition, and I went out with him to have soft drink and ice cream. I loved him very much. In summer times when he went to his birthplace (a nearby village), I used to send him love letters in colour envelopes. Once I wrote, "Where are you my dearest? I envy the moon that can see you every night but I cannot! I am asking the moon to convey my greetings and love to you!" I remember my letters were very compassionate and sometimes copy of love letters from magazines or books. His response was cool, he never said he loved me only said that he missed our being together. When sitting next to him I never dared to tell him that how much I wanted to have intimate relation with him. It was a taboo and I did not dare to express it. I am sure he knew my dirty thoughts, but never said anything or never refused me. No one could be better than I was for him. Private tuition, nice food in our house and spending money on him who was from a rather poor family where all opportunities he could not get anywhere else. Those three years I studied hard. In the first year, I had to wear glasses, as my eyesight was getting worse. I was among the first five students of the high school. My only hobby was to be with my boyfriend! Later when I heard he had a younger sister I wished that I could see his sister, and wished I could marry his sister; however, I never told him my feelings about his sister and did not tell my parents either. I even did not ask what his sister's name was. I remember in one of my letters to him I had written, give my regards to your family and sister as well. In response, he did not mention anything, so I thought I had made a rude expression and never again, mentioned anything about his sister.

One of my memories in last year of my study in high school, which shows how fool I was, is as follows. In a summer time when we were in the countryside, my twin brothers were breast-fed from a young woman. She was rather plump and nice looking about 26 years old. She had big firm breasts and when feeding my brothers did not hide her breasts from my eager looks. I must say that in those days in my country when women were feeding their children, usually they did not hide their breasts, only some covered their breasts under their hijabs or put a scarf on their chests as to hide their breasts, which was usually full of milk. It was an accepted thing and usually passer-byes did not stare at them or tell them off. I had seen several times in the main streets of my hometown that beggars sitting on the pavement breast-feeding their children showing off their breasts intentionally to attract men to give them some money. However, I think she rather swung them intentionally to attract me. I remember I blushed and turned away my face. I never tried to talk to her if in case we were left alone and never imagined she wanted to be intimate with me. Only I imagined having intimate relation with her when I was alone or sleeping. Later in the autumn when we returned to town, she brought her young sister who was then 16 years old to our house and said she could work as a house cleaner. My mother said her brother needed a house cleaner and soon they arranged to send her to The Capital to work for them. My uncle's wife had given birth to a new child and they needed an extra worker. They had a chauffeur and a gardener. The wife of the gardener was their cook. My eldest uncle was a rich man living in a big house. Any way this girl was sent to The Capital. She promised to be a good girl. She worked for my uncle for about 18 months. Then she was sent back to us. My uncle had said she had tried to attract his chauffeur. I remember when she was sent back, I was in the last year of high school. I was studying hard aiming for the university. I used to concentrate on the subjects I was studying; reading them repeatedly or trying to solve maths and physics problems. As soon as I could not concentrate, my thoughts would diverge from books and go to sexual problems; I would usually think of handsome boys specially my boyfriend, I seldom thought about girls or women. In our society in the fifties talking to women other than close relatives was taboo, so thinking about them was forbidden at least for me. When this young girl came to our home to work for us and help my mother who had then six children and was pregnant expecting a new child, we were all glad. She used to wear a hijab and was told not to show off and talk to the men in the house. Another man in the house was our cook who I have talked about him before. I had noticed that she was very interested to talk to him or me or in case to a man coming to our house to help gardening. I remember one evening about 5 p.m. my mother and the house cleaners were washing clothes at a corner of our garden made especially for washing clothes. Those days washing machine was not available in our hometown or perhaps we had not heard of it. I was going towards my mother to ask for something to eat. I saw the young and beautiful girl who had some washed clothes in a basket bringing to hang them on a rope. She was going away from other women and was coming towards me. I noticed that as I got close to her she started smiling at me; as she had the basket of clothes in her hands, her hijab was loose on her. I stared at her for a moment. For the first time since she had come to our house, I could see her body under hijab. She was wearing a blue top while I could see how tight it was for her; because I could see her firm breasts with its sharp nipples. It was the most beautiful creature I had seen by then. Her beautiful face with large black eyes and pretty lips was smiling at me. She asked me if I wanted anything. Instead of thanking her and saying something such as some bread and butter, I said if I wanted something to eat, I would rather ask from my mother! I thought it was a great sin to keep looking at her and keep talking to her, so I got myself out of the situation. Now I think how disappointed she was for talking to me or trying to attract me towards herself. About a month later when the weather was cold and other members of the family went to bed at 9 p.m. or by the latest at ten o'clock, I used to study until midnight in my room. I had a room of my own, which was my bedroom and my studying room. One night about midnight, I heard a knock on the door. I was deeply thinking about a maths problem and perhaps had abused myself earlier in the evening. It was after that bad habit that I could concentrate hard and solve difficult problems. Any way to my surprise, this young girl was on the doorstep with a glass of water in her hands. I asked her why she disturbed me and interrupted me from studying. I remember her eyes as if she had woken after a long sleep; her dress was open fronted and as women in those days didn't wear bras, I could see a part of her firm beautiful breasts as if bursting out of her dress. She was so sexy and I think she had prepared herself to seduce me but I did not notice her intention. She said she thought I had called for a glass of water and that was why she was there. Again, I told her rudely that who needs water in a winter midnight. She said she was sorry she had disturbed me and soon disappeared. Now when I remember this I say to myself how fool I was. I could have at least talked to her; and perhaps had a kissing session with her not going very far. That time I had heard that some house cleaners had sex relation with the property owner or his sons and if the house cleaner got pregnant, they had to marry her. Four months later in spring, she and our servant who was originally a Negro left our house secretly. The servant was about 60 years old at the time he left and the pretty girl only 18. After a month, we heard that she was left with no money and so she had become a prostitute. A lorry driver took her to The Big City and as she was young and beautiful, almost all lorry and taxi drivers had gone to her house in the prostitute's alley and had sex with her. Her cousin married her although he was already married in order to take the poor girl out of the house; He had made this sacrifice just to save her from being abused.

Our society was very religious. Presumably, all men and women were supposed to be clear of any kind of sins but there were some outrageous men or women in our closed society. I remember a young man, who was the son of one of our house cleaners. He was a rude boy and soon was addicted to opium and lived in the house of a prostitute. He became a pimp! Afterwards, he married this woman, brought her to his mother's house, and lived with her ever after. His wife gave birth to a daughter who had a forced marriage at the age of fourteen because had gone out with a boy and had lost her virginity. Even their daughter, brought up in a closed society was outrageous by instinct I think. This shows that you could find both men and women in that sacred society who did not confine themselves with customs.

My youngest sister was born in March 1963. Beginning of June that year, I was taking my last year exams. One of the exams was trigonometry. One of the questions was the hardest ever. No one had answered it right. Later when in England, I gave it to our maths teacher to see if he could solve it. He attempted different ways to prove the relationship but he never came to the solution.

In June 1963, I graduated from high school as the top student with highest average. My parents were very delighted. My eldest uncle told me he would take me with himself to the Tokyo Olympics scheduled in 1964. Rumours was spread that I had graduated with maximum average, although I found out later that someone else had obtained overall average more than me from a nearby village, however I enjoyed being known as the maths giant of the town. I was then preparing myself for the university entrance exam to be hold in August. I went to The Capital to go to language school.

After the final year exams in June, my father took us all to a holy city. We went to The Capital first by bus and then to the holy city by train. It was our first experience travelling by train. When we returned from the holy city, my parents stayed in The Capital for a few days. I was going to stay in The Capital until entrance exam day. That is until the day for universities entrance exam. Now when in my grandfather's house we met my other uncle who had returned from UK for his summer holidays. I had four uncles. The eldest uncle was my mother's brother from the same mother. The other three were in fact my half-uncles. The one who was two years older than I was; my grandfather had sent him to UK at the age of 15. He was humorous and kinder to us more than his brothers and his sister (my step aunt). My eldest uncle told my parents that he would find a grant for me to study abroad. In fact, he had some friends in some organizations and later he said I could go to Beirut to study in American University of Beirut and my expenses during my studies would be paid. A big opportunity I missed! When my half-uncle heard this, he said it is not good. As he has been the top student in his hometown, he should go to England. In the meantime, he told me how much English girls loved young men from Eastern countries. He told me as soon as you get to London you will be surrounded by British girls. He exaggerated so much that I imagined as soon as I get there some girls would ask me to spend the night with them! My dreaming about girls and having good time with them was already high; these speeches made it worse. Therefore, I wanted to go to England for my university studies. Later my eldest uncle informed me that he had a friend in Sweden Embassy, who could send me over to Sweden to study Food Processing with a grant. He said this is a very good subject. He said when you finish your studies; he would employ me in advance. He owned a village and had a big agricultural business. This was very exciting offer! Enjoying free education and being employed in advance. When my half-uncle heard this, he again told me off. He said Sweden is a very cold place; besides they do not speak English. You must go to a country where their native language is English, besides do not forget what I told you about English girls. Therefore, he put me off again and I was insisting to go to England no matter what. The university entry exam was held in two sessions. The first one was in early July for general subjects. I passed the first exam all right while my competitor from high school did not. One day he came to me and said his father was going to send him abroad to continue his studies. This made me not to bother much about the second entry exam, which was more advanced. I attempted for Mechanical Engineering. I was rather perverted. I showed as if I was a very studious student and a clean boy while I must confess that I was sexually depressed! I used to go to the language school in city centre by bus. I remember once there was a big queue, I hesitated until a young girl got on the bus. I followed her and stood behind her. The bus was overloaded. I was very close to her and in one occasion when the bus made an emergency break, I nearly fell over her. I could feel her buttocks and I tried to grab her hard pretending I had no other choice. The poor girl groaned and frowned at me. When I think about this and when I remember the poor girl's face I become ashamed of myself. How stupid I was! In an occasion when my uncle had taken me to his villa at seaside, I remember once in the afternoon about 3 p.m. when everybody was having an afternoon nap, I walked along the beach. In nearby I found two young girls lying on the beach sun bathing. They had taken off their bras. One of them was lying on her belly while the other one was lying on her back. I walked around them for a while. Seeing naked slim bodies with their breasts showing gave me an instant excitement. I do not know if they noticed me or not, even if they did they pretended to be asleep or perhaps were waiting for me to make a pass on them. I was very shy, unsociable and foolish indeed. Talking to girls was a taboo for me. I just walked around for a few minutes, and then returned to the villa being very frustrated. How fool I was. Why should I abuse myself if I did not dare to talk to the girls?

CHAPTER 3

1-3 My studies abroad

When the second university exam results were announced, I was not accepted. I insisted that I wanted to go to England to continue my studies. My dear father agreed and said he would do anything for me, although studying abroad would be very expensive but he would do his best to send me money and other expenses. Now I understand how expensive was studying in England and how much he sacrificed for me. Anyway, I asked my half-uncle to send me a letter of acceptance. He left early September and in two weeks' time, I had the letter of acceptance from a college where he was reading for 'A' levels. He was in his final year at that college and he knew the headmaster of the college. It took about two months to get passport and visa from the British Embassy in The Capital. It was early November that I set off for Heathrow Airport in London. My grandfather had sent him a telegram and told him the date and time of my arrival. They told me he would come to the airport and fetch me to his flat on my arrival, but they wrote his address on a piece of paper just in case he did not come to the airport. In the airport, my parents came to convoy me. In addition, my eldest uncle was there. He had bought a pair of handmade rugs as a gift and told me in case you ran out of money sell them. My mother was crying a lot. I had tears in my eyes and left them while I was very sad. I was searching for my fate. The flight was with Pan American Airways. It stopped in Beirut and those going to London had to change the flight. In the plane there were two Americans sitting next to me. I did not talk to them and did not ask where they were going. I thought as they were foreigners most probably they were going to London. Therefore, I followed them in Beirut Airport. They took their bags and went out. I followed them. An officer asked me how long I was going to stay in Beirut, I said only one night! I am going to London I said. I asked him for my suitcase, he told me to wait until it arrives. About an hour passed, then a flight hostess was running and shouting a London passenger is lost. He asked the officer if he had seen anybody. He showed me, the hostess took my hands and told me to run fast. She said the plane was kept waiting for me and said she was lucky she had found me. Otherwise, the plane had left and I had to stay in Beirut without my suitcase until the next flight. My speaking was very poor. It was my first trip abroad and being shy and inexperienced made it worse. When we got to London Airport, I showed the officer my passport and letter of acceptance. I told him my uncle was supposed to come to the airport and fetch me. They paged his name many times but there was no response. They kept me in the airport for about two hours, then they gave me one-month visa and the officer told me I must apply for student visa as soon as I register at the college. Soon I found out that my half-uncle had not come to the airport to fetch me. Therefore, I called a taxi and gave him the address, which was written on a piece of paper. When arrived at my uncle's flat it was about 10p.m. I had a few five-pound notes and some travel checks with me. I asked how much I should pay. I paid him a five-pound note and he gave me some silver back. I think he charged me too much because he soon noticed I did not know much about their currency. Never mind, I rang the bell and my uncle came to the door and said oh dear I forgot to come to the airport. I went upstairs and he showed me to a room. It was a small room with a bed inside. I put my suitcase there. He told me I could sleep there. We went to the lounge. There was his cousin who was a very handsome boy perhaps a couple of years older than I was. My half-uncle brought some food for me and after a while, he said they were going out to a nightclub and told me to go to bed. He said you must be tired and we will talk about your college tomorrow. I went to the bedroom. I could not see much from the windows. Soon I fell asleep. It was a hard day's night! I woke up about 6 a.m. I did my praying. I noticed that my uncle and his cousin were fast asleep. I went to bed again, woke up about 8 a.m. I noticed they were fast asleep! I was getting hungry and wanted something to eat but I was shy and did not dare to look around and find something to eat. I came back to my room and looked out at the window. I was surprised to see buildings all black. In addition, I noticed taxis were black and had special feature. Some cars that passed by were mostly black and small. In The Capital, American cars were mostly in the streets. Also taxis were Mercedes Benz. There were no British cars in my country; besides most cars had different colours other than black. To me it appeared very strange. How come London The Capital of England seemed to have very old buildings and to me old cars! In my thoughts, London was a modern city with big cars and wide streets. Any way about 1.p.m my uncle and his cousin got up while spreading their hands out and yawning. They later dressed up and said let's go and eat something. We came to the street. Round the corner there was a restaurant called Golden Egg. My uncle ordered three stakes. In there I was staring at the maid. She was a pretty girl wearing a red blouse with a yellow skirt as I remember. My uncle said, "you see I told you the girls here are very pretty and are in fund of coloured men!" For a moment, I thought he was going to invite her to his flat in the evening and what a night it would be. Nothing happened. After lunch, we went to the flat. My uncle said it is Sunday today and we cannot do anything except watching television. Later he said, "I think it is better for you to go to a language school and study language this year rather than going to the college". He said it was late for me to go to the college he was studying that time of the year. I told him I did not know much about studies in England and I would do whatever he recommends. On Monday morning, we went to some English language institutions in London. He also got phone number of some other institutes. Some said they had started their courses and some were very expensive as my uncle said. When back at home he said there is a language school in Brighton, which is a boarding school too. He asked me how much I had with me; I think I had enough money for three months lodging and registration fees. The next day he took me to Paddington Station and sent me off to Brighton. He told me someone would come to the station and fetch me to the school. In the train, I was in a compartment. I had my rugs and a suitcase. There were two old women sitting in front of me. One of them said you have beautiful rugs. She said "are these Persian rugs?" I said no! They had not heard the name of my country and I did not know where Persia was! I tried to tell them where my country was. They looked at me gloomily and I think we did not understand each other. I had my own language accent and they had their own English accent. About 2p.m. the train stopped in Brighton which was the last stop. I got off the train. A man in his fifties held the writing: International Language School of Brighton in his hands. I went towards him and introduced myself. He introduced himself as Mr Thompson. He looked very serious. He welcomed me to Brighton and showed me the way to his van. It was a red van with sliding doors. We soon arrived at the boarding school. He took me to a room in which there were four beds. He also took me to the school, which was not far away and introduced me to the headmaster. They were called Mr and Mrs Bryant as I remember. Mrs Bryant was a very pleasant woman gave me some forms to fill in and asked for the registration fees. She told me that I could start from next day. In the boarding house, Mr Thompson and his wife who looked more pleasant introduced me to some of the students and especially to my roommates. They said they would ring the bell for dinner. I was very hungry and could not wait for the dinnertime. Finally, at 6.30 p.m. they rang the bell and many students started running towards the dining room. There was a big table with about forty seats around it. I sat and waited for Mrs Thompson to give permission to start. In my front, there was a plate full of mashed potatoes, some beans and carrots. Also, there was a small piece of thin meat. I did not like the taste of the food at all but as I was very hungry, I ate it reluctantly. Mrs Thompson noticed that and said I understand you; no wonder you do not like English food but soon you will get used to it. Any way my life started in Brighton. The next day I went to the school, which was round the corner at 8 a.m. just after the breakfast. To my surprise, it was closed. I rang the bell; someone appeared at the door and told me the school starts at 9 o'clock. I noticed later that she was a cleaner.

2-3 My stay in Brighton November 1963-July 1964

I do not remember much else about my first days in the school. It took about two weeks before I met some boys from my country at the school. The students were mostly from Middle East countries, Turkey, Lebanon, Saudi Arabia, Jordan, Israel and some African countries. There were also a few students from European countries especially from Iceland, Norway, Finland, Germany and Greece. The first few months I felt very lonely and I used to cry when I went to bed in the evenings. I really had missed my parents and my friends. Soon I found out that all those things my half-uncle had told me about British girls were wrong. No one ever asked how I was. Later in the school some school mates told me not to worry so much and said some jokes to make me laugh. I met a compatriot student who was a very handsome looking boy. I noticed that in the school many girls had an eye on him. I tried to make friends with him and soon I found out that he was very friendly with me. He told me not to worry so much and one day took me to the YMCA where I met four other compatriots. One day I told him I fancied a dish of rice and meat. He told me there is an Indian Restaurant in Brighton which served rice. I got the address and got myself to the restaurant one evening at 6p.m. I missed the dinner of the boarding house. I had a big aspiration to eat a home dish after so many months. It was a small restaurant newly established at a bottom of a road near the Brighton University campus. It was lighted with red lamps, a gloomy place with no one in it. An Indian waiter came to me and gave me the menu. My friend had told me to order chicken curry. I showed him chicken curry on the menu, and then he asked mild or hot. I told him very hot. He looked at me strangely. I didn't know why. Later he brought the food for me. A plate full of rice with a small dish looked blackish with a chicken leg and a thick curry sauce. I was glad to see it. After so many months I was going to eat something similar to our traditional food. I put some curry sauce on the rice and also a bit of meat. I took it vigorously to my mouth. It was so hot I mean in the taste that soon my tears came out. I had never eaten such a hot meal before in my life. I think it was made of red chilli and it was the hottest curry they had in Indian restaurants. I was swearing and cursing my friend. Never mind, I had to pay for it so I ate the lot gradually. It cost me a pound I remember which was a lot of money those days. A pound was twenty shillings and a shilling was twelve pence. So a pound was 240 pence. A penny was a big copper coin. The paper money was one pound and five pound notes. Later they introduced ten pound notes as well. On my return to the boarding school I saw my friend and told him about the Indian restaurant. He laughed at me and said next time order mild curry. By hot they mean hot in taste something full of pepper!

After three months, Mr Thompson told me they have new students coming to the boarding house, he said I should go and stay with a family. The family they introduced was not far from the school. They were a pleasant retired couple. I cannot remember their names. They gave me a room on the second floor next to their bedroom. There was another room downstairs given to an Iraqi boy. Gradually I became friendlier with some school mates. I tried to talk to girls as well. There were some Turkish students whom I liked to tease them and talk to them. One day I talked to few English school girls aged 14-15 years old. They were walking along the street; I stopped and asked the language school address from them. I pretended I didn't understand what they were saying, of course they talked slang. There were some birds flying over the river alongside the street. I told them what these birds are called? They said we are birds as well aren't we beautiful. I said "Oh no, you are not birds, you are school girls". They insisted to tell me that girls in slang are called birds. Of course I understood what they meant but I wanted to tease them intentionally. They kept talking to me and at the end; I invited them for a cup of tea at a tearoom, which served Ceylon Tea only, to come the next day. They turned up at the tea room and on the table I told them some jokes which made them laugh a lot, but that was it and I never saw them again.

My new boyfriend was an honest and handsome boy. I enjoyed being with him. In addition, I found another friend who was very kind. One Saturday evening, my friend told me he was going to a dancing club and took me with himself. It was my first time going to a club. It was on the second floor of a building. There was a bar and a girl behind the bar. The room was not so big, perhaps six by eight meters, but it was full of young boys and girls most of them were dancing to the Beatles' record. There was a drunken girl, whose buttons of her blouse was open and I could see her breasts out of her bra. It was very exciting for me to see naked breasts. A stranger came to us and said if we fancied having intimate relation with that girl. He said he would take us out in his car and pay one pound each and have sex relation with her. I was very delighted and agreed immediately. It was about 10 p.m. we rushed downstairs and the girl whose name was Peggy came after us. Stranger brought his car in front of us; it was a small black car. I sat in front; Peggy and my boyfriend sat in the back seat. He drove outside The Big Cityand after ten minutes got into a deserted road. All the way long my boyfriend was playing with Peggy, kissing her and enjoying himself. I wished I had sat in the back seat, although if I were there I wouldn't do anything. Driver told us to get out of the car and get with the job quickly. Peggy stayed in the back seat taking her clothes off, and then my boyfriend said he would go first. We turned our back to them while they were having sex relation. It was finished in a minute. Then it was my turn. We did not have preservative and had sex relation without preservative. It took me only a few seconds. I was very excited and having the bad habit of self- abusing had made me weak, I must say very weak indeed. I met Peggy several times afterwards. Once I took her to the cinema and kissed her a lot in the dark, played around with her while she was playing with me. Soon I wetted my trousers, I think some audience noticed that and I could hear someone groaning. We then left the cinema without waiting for the film to end. Peggy was a sex maniac; she went out with many boys and wished to get married. Some boys paid her and others just abused her. In another occasion, a school mate from language school told me to go to his flat. He said there are some other boys. When I arrived I saw four school mates. To my surprise, Peggy was lying on the bed naked. I had sex relation with her. I was ashamed that it didn't last at all. I had told myself a lot before and had sworn not to abuse myself but always had broken my promise after four or five days. Later I was warned not to go out with Peggy again. I was told she was a well-known prostitute and one may get skin disease from her. Therefore, I didn't go out with her anymore. The term in the school finished in June 1964. Before the end of the term, I was trying to make friends with Slovak girls. There was a beautiful Finish girl who was an easy pass as I had heard. One day in the class room I invited her to go out with her to the cinema or tearoom but she refused. She was in my dreams for a long while. In another occasion, a friend invited me to go to a park with him one afternoon. He said he had invited two Icelandic girls to come and he needs another company. It was about four p.m. that I met them in the park. The Icelandic girls were very beautiful, had a kind of green eyes with blond hair. We sat next to each other, while my friend was talking to one of them he insisted me to keep chat with the other one. Both girls were pretty and you couldn't prefer one to the other. After some time, my friend suggested to start walking along the park, soon he said let us run and chase each other. We kept running for about ten minutes, we then sat down while we were all breathing fast. When I sat down, I noticed my eyes were going black and my head was somehow dizzy and heavy. A few minutes later I started vomiting. I was so ashamed in front of these girls. Later he told me I must exercise every day. I pretended I had eaten too much. I didn't make a date with the Icelandic girl.

When the term ended, we were told to find accommodation for ourselves. I found a cheap bedsitter somewhere down town. The landlady gave me a room at the top floor (third storey). There were two beds in the room and she said she would let the other room as soon as she finds a tenant for it. It was quite cheap, two pounds ten shillings per week. In the cheap bedsitter I had a few interesting stories. Most evenings I went to a cafe with my handsome boyfriend and only asked for a sandwich. When it got crowded the bar man would ask us to leave, then we would order another soft drink and stay for another half an hour or so. Usually young foreign boys and girls would turn up and it was a place for making dates. One evening a Swedish girl came in, she had been drinking because she had a Brazilian boyfriend who apparently had left her and was going with someone else. She was swearing at this boy who was our school mate and we all knew him. Perhaps he had left England after the term had finished. About 11 p.m. the barman told us to leave the bar, he must close the bar. At those days bars were open until 11 p.m. The bar man said someone must take this drunken girl to her flat. No one accepted, a school mate told me to accompany her to her flat because he said we know you wouldn't harm her. I happily accepted the offer. Out of the bar, this beautiful Swedish girl was leaning on my shoulder and I carried her all the way to her flat. I could feel her warm body and how she let herself on me. I was excited very much, but I didn't dare to kiss her, never mind playing with her. I thought it would be a sin to abuse her. It was a very unforgettable memory for me. Later, I abused myself a lot with her dreams. I always regretted why I didn't kiss her. At front of her flat she opened the door and thanked me for taking her home. Another memory from the cafe was that one evening I was with my handsome boyfriend. A British girl came and asked if she could join us. We were both delighted. She got some beer and at the close of the bar she told my handsome boyfriend that she had fancied him and wanted to have sex relation with him. They came to my flat and made love to each other and they left before dawn! When they had gone, I abused myself as usual. I blamed myself why the girl didn't fancy me. Why I was so shy and again vowed not to abuse myself so much?

When in Brighton I did not have any news from my uncle who was then living in London. He was accepted by the London University to read Mechanical Engineering. In the year passed, he had finished his 'A' levels in Gloucester College. I didn't have his address although he had the Language school address, but he never wrote to me. I used to write a letter to my parents, it took about three weeks to get to my hometown and usually after about five or six weeks I would get a response. I had asked my father to send me memorial stamps instead of ordinary stamps. He did that and I have kept all the envelopes he has posted all the years I was in England. Unfortunately I have not kept the letters. It would have been a good reminder of my memories.

In Easter holidays my half-uncle came to Brighton for his holidays and also visiting me and a friend of him who was living in Brighton. He was a family friend, his father was partner of my uncle back home. I had met him in my uncle's house in the Capital. He was a tall fat man couple of years older than me. He was a humorous person, had always something to say and also jokes. His father had introduced a family resident in Brighton. My father would send my expenses in our currency to my uncle in The Capital and he would transfer it to Pounds in England via this family. The first time I went to his house, I found him and his wife very friendly. They had a beautiful daughter aged about sixteen. My fat friend boasted that he was going out with her. I told him she is too young how you dare going out with her. He said her parents didn't mind and if they agreed he would marry her. He did go out with her, but he never married her. Any way when my uncle came to Brighton, he took us for a ride in his sport car. It was a very small MG made only for two passengers. I had to sit behind bending myself. His friend was tall and fat could never fit himself in the small backspace. In the car he was boasting and telling a lot of lies about his sexual relation with British girls. My uncle boasted as well. Later he said there is a night club in Portsmouth not very far from Brighton. He persuaded my uncle to take us there. So he drove off to Portsmouth and we got to the club about 8 p.m. We had dinner and sat on a table near the stage. It was a small room, perhaps about six or seven tables were there; music was played from a gramophone from loudspeakers. Record players had not come to the market yet. After a while a man came to the stage and invited the guests for a striptease show. I was very excited. It was first time in my life seeing a dancer taking her clothes off gradually with music. A young woman danced with the music and started to take her clothes off piece by piece. She took her bra off and threw it to a corner of the stage, after a minute she pretended to take her pants off, but they turned the gloomy lights off and I was not able to see her all naked. My half-uncle then started boasting that this is nothing. He said there is a striptease club in Soho of London called GG club. He said not only the girls striptease and take everything off, even their pants but that in one occasion a girl masturbated on the stage! I was so simple to believe that! From that night it was my ambition to go to London and visit GG club and see how the girls masturbate on the stage! About 10:30 p.m. we returned to Brighton and my uncle drove off to London. He even didn't invite me to London. However, I was glad to have seen him after about six months or so and more was impatiently looking forward to going to London on my own. I had told a friend about GG club in London and he said if he goes to London, he would invite me.

2-3 My first visit to London

In the summer time my friend had gone to London and invited me to go and spend the weekend with him. I took a train and went to London. It was my first visit to London; He had told me how to get to his bed-sitter from the station. I remember it was in Edgware Road not too far from Marble Arch. I had agreed to pay for two nights I stayed with him. In this way he made a bargain! On Saturday afternoon he told me there is a place called Piccadilly in London, there are Striptease and night clubs there; he said GG club is in Soho which is nearby. I decided to go to Piccadilly but he didn't accompany me. I also didn't know which bus to take so I decided to go to Piccadilly by walk. He told me to go all the way along Oxford Road and then ask someone to show me the rest of the way. I walked for more than an hour before I got to Piccadilly. There were some striptease clubs and other kind of clubs. I walked around a lot until I found GG club. I went inside; a man asked if I was a member, I said no so he charged me one pound to get inside. It was a small room perhaps six by four meters. All the walls were painted red. The stage was red as well. There were only four rows of seats, and five chairs in each row. The club was half full and I sat in the third row. There was a music played very loud from a gramophone for that small place. The curtains were drawn and a pretty girl appeared on the stage. I couldn't see much her face in the darkened room, but soon she started dancing and taking her clothes off. I always remember the song with which the girl danced with while doing striptease; it was called 'the house of the rising sun' by the group called Animals. Apparently it was on the charts and very popular. This time the girl finally took her pants off but before you could see anything, she turned round and the curtains dropped. She didn't masturbate as my uncle had said. A few minutes later, another girl came in and danced striptease, I had already abused myself in the dark and wanted to get out quickly. The audience were mostly old men, perhaps one or

37

two foreigners as well. I then walked all the way back home. I got to the bed-sitter by midnight. My friend opened the door for me and I went to bed immediately. I was so tired that I fell asleep soon. On Sunday I returned to Brighton but thinking all the way how to go back to London again. I was told living in London was much more expensive than in Brighton. I only had fifty pounds per months, which was for my lodging and living.

3-3 Living in London July to August 1964

One day in August while the weather was quite warm, I remember about four p.m. suddenly there was a knock on the door and before I could reply, the door was opened. There stood my half-uncles at the door front. I was shocked to see them. They started teasing me saying oh we saw you masturbating. They had my Brighton address from my parents in my country. My youngest half-uncle, his mother and sister had come to London. My step aunt was pregnant and they had decided to come over and have her child born in London. My elder half-uncle who lived in London, had a big flat near Earl's Court metro station. That summer I did not go to my country. Instead, I stayed the whole vacation in London with them. He also had a MGB sport car. For the first time I learned how to get on metro trains. My step grandmother wanted me to accompany my youngest half-uncle who was a lazy student and didn't want to study. He had come to study in England just to be far away from his parents who were hurt by his behaviour and couldn't control him at all. His brother told me he had registered him in the same college as me to read 'O' levels while I would study for 'A' levels. I stayed with them in London for about two months. My time was wasted. I was ashamed to talk about girls with my youngest half-uncle who used to smoke a lot but not in front of her mother; outside the house or in the toilet! One day we were taken to Gloucester. He showed us the college and took us where he used to live himself the year before. We were supposed to live with a family whose house was only five minutes' walk from the college. It was up a road called East Road. The owners were in their fifties and had no children. Our room was on the second floor. It was a big room with 2 beds and a table inside. My youngest half-uncle and I were supposed to stay in this room. My schoolmate from my hometown had come to London as well later than me and had studied English in London. We were in contact with each other and he said he wanted to come and study 'A' levels with me in Gloucester. I asked the landlady to let a room also to him as well. When the term started, we were introduced to two other gays; a Greek student and a Scot engineer. My uncle knew the Scot man and they talked a lot. I was supposed to look after my youngest half-uncle, persuade him to study and teach him mathematics and other subjects.

4-3 My stay in Gloucester September 1964-June 1966

The Gloucester College was near The City centre. There was a cinema and some shops and the main bus stop in The City centre. I never took bus there because our home was quite near the college and city centre. The train station was not too far either and it took only one and a half hour to get to London by train. I cannot remember much about the first few months. The headmaster was very kin on me and had recognised me as a top student. My hometown friend was in a different class. My youngest half-uncle usually got up late, instead of getting to the college at 9 he would miss the first class and get there at 11. One day, headmaster told me: I understand your uncle is your roommate, how come he gets so late to the college? I said he has got a back ache! The class broke into laughter. He told me they would report his absence to his brother. When my uncle heard it he said he didn't like studying; he came here to enjoy himself! There were about five or six other students form my country. The first three were from rather rich families. Especially, one who had bought a Jaguar sport car. He was rich and handsome and most college girls wanted to become his girlfriend. He was very kind to me and soon he wanted me to help him in mathematics. After a few months studying in the college I became well known to be an expert in mathematics. In one occasion, our teacher had asked how we could find the roots of an equation he had proposed. I had said immediately that the roots could be found by drawing two lines on a same graph paper and locating their intersection. I gave him the answer in less than a minute. He was surprised for my quick response and from then on all my class mates admired me for understanding mathematics better than all of them. Soon I became friendly with all the students from my country. Unfortunately we didn't make any friends with local British students. The family used to give us breakfast and full dinner in weekends. It cost us five pounds per week. For heating there was an electric heater in our room, we had to put coins inside to get electricity for heating, and that was very expensive. The house owners trusted us specially me who was very quiet and was a hard working student. In the evenings we would go and watch TV in their sitting room. They didn't have any children. She said during the Second World War she was pregnant, but one day she had lost her parents in Nazi bombardments. By hearing that she had a miscarriage and since then she did not become pregnant any more. Her husband and she were opera singers and sometimes they practised singing church songs. They used to go to church every Sunday and sing with Organ in many occasions. They had a cat and were very fond of their cat. They had made a special place for their cat in front of the coal fire they had in the sitting room.

My youngest half-uncle was always thinking about girls; of course he was handsome and had more money than me, but whenever he got his money from his brother in London he would spend it quickly, say in a week and he would be without money for the rest of the month. As he was my half-uncle, I used to lend him money but later I refused and told him I needed myself. He had written a letter to his father and asked for more money. He used to get twice as much as me from his father. In Brighton, I was becoming friendlier with people, but unfortunately, in Gloucester I was feeling lonely, always ashamed of myself. Self-abusing was the only thing which relieved me from everything. I used to abuse myself two or three times a day. This had made me weak and fragile. Our meeting with my countrymen college mates gradually made me more talkative but still shy with the girls. In second year of my stay in Gloucester, I had learnt how to go to London during weekends. I remember first time I went to London, I went to London with a week- end return ticket. I stayed Friday night with my uncle. I went to Piccadilly in the evening and was wondering about when a man approached me and said if I liked to watch a blue film. I didn't understand what he meant, but I said yes how much is it? He said it costs two pounds. He took me to an old building, up the stairs and introduced me to a drunken man who led me to a small room. Only two rows of chairs were there. The room was dark and a film was shown on a small screen with a noisy projector. Everything was old, the chairs, the projector and I guess the film itself. The story was about a man in a hotel who had ordered dinner in his room. He was lying on the bed rubbing himself; as soon as the maid laid the try on the table for him, he attacked the poor girl and took her clothes off and forced her to obey him. The lovemaking went on fiercely while the girl tried to get out of his hands, but later she surrendered and seemed to be enjoying herself. The film was in black and white and the projector noise was so loud that we couldn't hear the music or the conversation of the actors. Only five people were there and I think all were masturbating. I tried a lot to hold myself but I wetted myself at last. After about an hour or so, I left. The man in charge asked me if I wanted to be with a model, it would cost you two pounds he said. I agreed and he led me upstairs and knocked on the door. An old lady opened the door and told me to get inside and wait for a while. A man came out of the bedroom and I was told to go inside. A young woman in her thirties was lying naked on the bed. She told me to get off my clothes and get on with it. I asked her if I could suck her breasts. She told me I could do so. It was my first time sucking a woman's breasts. I did it so harshly that she cried and said be gentle,' haven't you seen a woman before?' I stopped sucking and as soon as I wanted to have sex relation I had orgasm. It didn't even last a second. The girl got up and told me to put on my clothes and get out. I always remember this first occasion of my experience in London. From then on I used to go to London at least once a month and wonder in Piccadilly to find someone. They used to announce their presence by writing "young model" on their doors. Usually they cost two pounds. It was for a quick go. There was a nice tall woman who charged two pounds but she even didn't undress, just pulled down her jeans and did not allow me to get undressed either. Everything was finished in a minute or two. One night I came across a young model that apparently had started business very recently. She charged five pounds but she was very beautiful and kind to me. Her name was Valerie and I used to visit her for quite a long period. Once she sent me a letter giving me her new address. My house mate asked who was it and I told him I use to visit Valerie in London and pay her five pounds. He said he would like to see her as well. On a Saturday we bought a day return ticket and went to London. Then asked a policeman where Sheppard's Market was. He told us how to get a bus from Piccadilly and how to get there. My friend and I got there in time and found Valerie's flat all right. She welcomed us; I went to her bedroom first and told her about my friend. I was there for about five minutes but he stayed for about two minutes. Later he was groaning that five pounds was too much for just a few minutes. He was right!

In July 1965 I was very eager to go home for summer holidays. Therefore, as soon as the term ended I bought a return ticket by help of my uncle in London and set off for my country. I cannot remember much about that summer. Only that I had bought a suit case full of souvenirs for all of my family. Some expensive clothing and especially a big bottle of after shave from the airport shop. I had paid eight pounds for it which was very expensive; I think ordinary ones were about a pound only. My father blamed me for spending so much money on souvenirs. I was in the village with my family most of that summer. Back in The Capital before returning to England, I visited the so-called 'Dirty Suburb' twice.

When back in England I returned to the same family and stayed there for another year. This year was very important for me; I should sit for my 'A' levels and if obtained good results could choose a good university. I had already selected my field of study; I wanted to study Mechanical Engineering. That was a top engineering subject in the sixties. We had a physics teacher who wasn't very good but my maths teachers were quite good. I sat for 'A 'level exams in three subjects: pure and applied mathematics and physics in January. I obtained two grade A's and an E in Physics. I had applied for three universities: Imperial College of London, University of Swansea and University of Sheffield. I was invited for interview by the first two universities. My interview with Imperial College was a disaster, I don't know why. I either gave wrong answers or hesitated too much. At the end of interview I was told to get three grade A's and also Ordinary degree in English. I had obtained Cambridge Certificate in English but presumably it wasn't sufficient. I also went to Swansea for interview. I had arrived there late in afternoon. I had to stay the night in a hotel. There was a hotel just outside the station and I went in and asked for a room. The man in charge was a very kind Irish man. He took me inside his room gave me a cup of tea and talked a lot about Irish hospitality. On next day I went to the Mechanical Engineering department of University of Swansea which was by the seaside and had a very nice view. In answering questions I flattered and had a delay in making correct sentences. Probably being in touch with my countrymen students in Gloucester and speaking in my own language most of the time had caused my speaking worse than when I was in Brighton. Anyway they told me I must sit for 'O' level in English but were happy about my grades in maths and physics. In the evening, I went to the hotel to get my staff and return to Gloucester. The Irish man wanted to keep me for another night and show me sightseeing's of Swansea, but I didn't agree. Therefore, I registered for these exams in June.

In another occasion when I was looking for a young model in Piccadilly I came across with a model who asked for ten pounds. That was plenty of money for a model in those days; but I decided to see this model. So I agreed to pay her. I was lead into the second storey of an old building. When I went inside and was told to get undressed I saw a very beautiful woman who was naked and was lying on her stomach on a single bed. She was the most beautiful woman I had ever seen by that time, a bit tall with full breasts and nice buttocks. Her skin was as if she had just come from seaside and had a sun bathing. She was so beautiful that I kept staring at her for some time. She then ordered me to get on with it. She just kept still while helped me to make love to her. It lasted only less than a minute and then I got dressed slowly while couldn't keep my eyes off her body. I paid ten pounds and left. I tried to come to this building a few times more but not only she wasn't there but there was no other model there either.

My visit to London's young models continued and I used to go to London at least once a month. In one occasion when I was returning to Gloucester, I met a beautiful girl who asked me where I was born. She said we were from same country and then she started conversation with me. I told her I was studying in Gloucester College reading for 'A' levels. As soon as she heard that, she smiled and said if I knew that rich boy. I said I was very friendly with him. She turned out to be his girlfriend who had come from The Capital recently. Later my rich friend took me to Oxford to meet his girlfriend, we became very friendly afterwards and I used to go to their house very often. Once he invited me to London. He had rented a luxury furnished flat in North London nearby a beautiful Park, which I cannot remember, its name. I think he was paying one hundred pounds per month for the rent; he also had a big Jaguar sport car. He had married his girlfriend formally. They took me to a posh cinema in Piccadilly, which was showing the film My Fair Lady.

Before going to the theatre ordered dinner. He said have you ever had poached eggs and I said no; so he ordered poached eggs for us. When I saw that, I was very surprised to see it! It was boiled egg on a piece of toast. However, it was nice and we enjoyed both the dinner and the film, which was indeed a classic musical film.

In June I sat for exams also sat for special exam in pure mathematics. I had received a notification for the dates of all the exams. For the English test, the date was set for on a Wednesday at 11 a.m. On Tuesday night my friends came to my room and asked me why I was absent for the English test. I showed them the notification I had and said the exam is on Wednesday. But they said the date of exam had been changed and displayed on the notice board. The next day I went to the registrar of the college and said I was not aware of the change in the exam date and asked if I could take the exam then. She ringed London and asked from the head office and they didn't allow me to take the exam. They said the questions were taken out of the exam room and it was my problem. I was very heartbroken. I was sure I would pass the test alright. I had already got the Cambridge Certificate in English when I was in Brighton and had prepared myself for the exam. All my hopes to get to Imperial College were vanished!

My relation with my half-uncle who was my roommate as well in the second year of my stay in Gloucester was not so good. He always wanted to enjoy himself while was a burden for me to study or to feel free. There was always a kind of restriction between me and him. One night a college girl called Carol came to my room about six p.m. She had come to see my rich friend who had a Jaguar sport car, and apparently, she was a bit drunk. I also bought beer for her but I soon found she was not kin on me. My half-uncle arrived later and told me to go to TV room so that he could have sex relation with her. Later I heard as if something dropped from the bed! It was my half-uncle; he wanted to have sex with her by force but she had used karate and dropped him off the bed. Afterwards always he said that he had sex relation with Carol and it was I who could not do anything. In another occasion one afternoon about four o'clock a very beautiful girl called Linda came to see me. It was a Tuesday afternoon and usually my rich boyfriend came to my flat on Tuesday evenings. I told Linda that I am expecting him to come and see me soon. She said she had come from Oxford; had heard about my rich friend from her friends and wanted to see him only. She said she could stay for a couple of hours and she should return to Oxford by eight o'clock. She asked if she could stay in my room until he arrives and I gladly agreed. She said she was very tired and wanted to sleep for a while; then she lied on my bed and soon fell asleep. She was wearing a short skirt and when asleep I could see her beautiful legs and even her thighs and buttocks. Her body figure was stunning; imagine a beautiful young girl of age sixteen with a very pure glorious innocent looking. She was so beautiful that I could not keep gazing away from her body while admiring her beauty all the time until she woke up after an hour or so. I just cannot describe how excited I was. When she finally woke up and saw that my friend had not arrived she left the house and thanked me for keeping her. She never came to my flat again and I never saw her in the college either. She had come from long way just to get friends with a rich and handsome boy! A rare opportunity for me; which happens once in a lifetime to enjoy presence of a young beautiful girl in my room alone. I never forget this memory; she was much more beautiful than that exceptional model I had met in London. I always regret why I didn't make a pass on her; however I am sure that she only wanted to be friends with that rich boy and no one else. Even then I was very shy and gazing at her beautiful body for more than an hour while she was asleep was more than enough for me. I didn't take my eyes off her even for a second. Sometimes she turned around and in that case, her skirt was rolled upwards; I just admired her beauty. She was so beautiful that I am not able to describe it. She had hazel brown hair and brown eyes. She was only sixteen and in that age she was looking so fresh and innocent that is beyond imagination. I was excited most of the time but I was not very enthusiastic to hold her or waken her up and chat with her. I thought it would be a sin to make a pass on her; after all she was eager to see my friend and not me.

5-3 My stay in London September 1966-October 1966

Before I went for my summer holidays to my country in July 1966, I received an acceptance letter from University of Sheffield. I was accepted to study for BSc degree in Mechanical Engineering. Among ten of my countrymen students in Gloucester College, only my schoolmate and I were accepted for BSc; my other friends were either accepted for HND or not accepted at all. The rich boy and another friend were accepted for HND all the others were not accepted anywhere; they either returned home or went to USA or Canada to try their luck. In fact entering to British Universities in the sixties was not as easy as it was later in late seventies or afterwards. In my hometown, we went to the village in summer time and I enjoyed the weather, the sound of singing birds in early mornings and waterfalls and the fresh fruits and organic foods more than anything else. For me it looked like a paradise. Now when I remember all those beautiful sceneries, excellent weather in the middle of desert and all those fresh and delicious fruits, it reminds me of description of heaven in our poetry books. Now in old age and in modern days when we go to the same village, I do not find any of those things. The air is now polluted because of so many cars coming into a closed village; there is a shortage of water although water is fed into houses by lead pipes. There is electricity and telephones everywhere. Anyway, having nothing much to do while eating good food and enjoying good weather in that summer holiday brought wrong doings that is self- abusing.

In one occasion, we went to visit my mother's relative wife and her daughter who was named to me by her late father. She was then sixteen years old; a beautiful girl whom I desired to be my future wife. Her mother welcomed my mother and me and in our visit that lasted about an hour or so, I talked to my fiancé to be for a short time. They asked me about my studies only and admired me for becoming a university student. I returned to London a month before the term started. On my return I had decided to attend a language school and sit for an advanced course in English. I rented a bedsitter in Bayswater for five pounds a week. It was on the fourth floor of an old building. I told the landlady I needed it for six months; since no one rented a room for less than six months but most of them knew it was for a short term rent. I then registered in a language school which was in Oxford Street. I cannot remember the name of the school, but I remember that the teacher was a very kind and knowledgeable person. He even knew many other languages and in one occasion, he explained a grammar rule to me in my own language. I was amazed very much and always respected him and the way he taught. In the school, there were few students from my country as well. Among them was a young girl who had come to London with her family. She was kind, shy but very attractive. I became friends with her and in break time, we talked a lot. Once I invited her to come to cinema with me; she accepted but didn't turn up. Later she said that she lived with her parents and they did not allow her to go out with boys. I always remember her kind reception. I went to Sheffield on the first day of October. I had asked a family to live with and they had booked a family in Whitley nearby Sheffield for me.

Conclusion

In the first year of my stay in England, I was gradually getting familiar with girls, but in Gloucester, I returned to my isolated and depressed situation badly. Perhaps presence of my half-uncle was a big excuse for me to hinder my ambitions grows naturally. Self-abusing made me shy, isolated, quiet, unsociable, unhappy depressed and miserable. I abused the best years of my life.

6-3 My stay in Sheffield October 1966-November 1970

I went to Kings Cross station in London to take a train to Sheffield. I arrived in Sheffield about 6 p.m. and I took a local train straight away to Whitley. It was forty-five minutes journey. When I got to the station, I gave the family address to a taxi driver. I had a big suitcase with me. It was only a few minutes away from the station. It was located somewhere close to the station. It was quite dark when I got there and rang the bell. A woman in her fifties welcomed me to the door and took me to a three-bedded room. She then told me to go to the dining room and gave me a cup of tea. There were also two British boys named John and Jeff. She also showed me a big room as our joint study room. I went to bed about ten o'clock and asked the English boys to help me in the morning for going to the University for Registration. We set off for the station about 8 a.m. and as soon as I got out of the house I were surprised to see a river just on the other side of the road! I told John look there is a river! He looked at me strangely and said didn't you know we were so closed to this river? I then realised that all the sound I heard in midnight, which awakened me from sleep, was from the river. We went to Sheffield University, which was fifteen minutes' walk away from the station. We were guided to a building for registration. The building was quite new. Actually, most of the university buildings were new. It was known as King's College and was expanded by new departments and buildings and changed to a big university. Later when we were handed some take-home homework we noticed the King's College logo on the sheets. The registration took about three hours. There was a long queue of fresh student's boys and girls. There was no sign of hurriedness and they took a photo of us and gave us a university Identity card. They told us there would be a tour of the University on the next day. We were then left alone to go home. Next day I attended our department, which was actually a luxury building. Some corridors were painted purple. There were big amphitheatres and large newly equipped laboratories. The head of department gave a nice lecture to the newcomers. On Wednesday, I went to the church to see an opening ceremony. It was my first visit to a church and I think I was the only person from Middle East to be present in the church. I was given a notebook of holy songs but I pretended I was singing the verses with other audiences. Later I went to shopping centre and opened a bank account. I looked around the city centre and found out where big stores were also I looked for bookies! I spent the few next day's idly. When the term started, I attended all my classes and studied hard. I even studied during weekends and seldom had a spare time. Only some afternoons after my classes I attended bookies and made a bet on horses. Usually I lost my money but this was my only hobby. During the first year, I visited Valerie in London twice I think. I went to London during weekends and stayed the nights in my uncle's flat. He was kind to me but never took me to a nightclub or dancing. He had found a new girlfriend and was happy going out with her. As long as he let me spend the night in his flat, I was satisfied. In one occasion, he took me to Kings Cross station and asked a passer-by to take a photograph of us. I had this photograph for many years. In June, the exams arrived so soon. I failed three subjects: Electronics, Metallurgy and Physics. I had thought the exams would start later, I had not seen the notice board on time and so I was not really prepared for the exams although I had studied hard during the year. My grade in maths was full mark. When I went to see my supervisor, he was astonished and said why I did not choose mathematics to study. I told him I have now found out that I understand mathematic much better than electronics and I would not mind changing my subject. He advised me to finish BSc in Mechanical Engineering and sit for MSc degree in Applied mathematics. He said this is a new department taking postgraduate students only. In the second year exams, I also failed electronics so I had to do an ordinary degree course.

In the summer of 1967, I went home once again. On my return, I decided to rent a bedsitter in Sheffield. I went to the accommodation office of the University and filled a form for the house of lodgings. I was told I would be informed as soon as there was a vacancy. I was given the address of a cheap bedsitter. I found the address and moved to this room. It was a furnished room with a double bed on the first floor of a two-storey building. The owner was an Indian who owned a hotel and told me he rarely comes to his house. He had kept a room for himself on the first floor. There were two other clients on the second floor. They were from Nigeria and I seldom met them. I stayed in this address from October until mid-January when I moved to the house of lodgings. On a Saturday night, I had gone to University's dancing club and returned home at about 11 p.m. As I was not familiar with the address, as soon as I got off from the bus, I saw a young woman standing there. I asked her if she could show me how to get to my home, she said she didn't know and told me off. I noticed a car stopped and she said something to the chauffer and got on the car and left. I asked someone else and found my way home all right. However, the behaviour of this girl made me wonder if she was a prostitute. So on next evening when just it was getting dark, I came out and walked across the street towards the bus station I had got off the night before, looking for wondering girls. I noticed a young woman with a white fur coat and strong cosmetics was walking by. I got close to her and asked if she would like to have a cup of coffee with me. She gladly accepted and we walked all the way to my flat. She asked me if I did business and when I asked for explanation, she said she meant sex relation. I gladly said yes and she said it would cost me two pounds! While tea was made, she took off her dress and we had sex relation together. It was a quickie as usual. Her stay lasted about fifteen minutes and I asked her to come to my flat on Wednesday night. She came to see me every two or three days and I was quite happy that I had found someone to relieve my enthusiasm with her. Each time after seeing her or self- abusing, I could concentrate and study for a couple of hours. After a couple of weeks, I decided to look for other girls. So, I started wondering in the streets and each time I went out I found a new woman. I had noticed that they came out between 8 to 10 p.m. Some of them had their own flats and some would come to my room. In one occasion, I went to the flat of a nice woman. The weather had just become cold. She had a coal fire and her room was cosy and warm. She undressed on her double bed and told me to get on with it. However, she had a small dog lying on the bed next to her. The dog was sleeping and snoring, I told the woman that I could not sleep next to a dog. She had a rocking chair in front of the fire; she told me to sit on the rocking chair and then she came on top of me. In this way, I couldn't see the dog and it was a nice memorable event for me. Next time I went to see her she had moved from that address. In another occasion, I went to a girl's house. She was a nice and young girl. I asked her why she did business and she said because her mother was ill and she was short of money. I did not see her again either. In mid-December before the Christ-mass holidays, two events happened. One evening I just got off from the bus, I went to a fish and chips shop. I was with a friend who was some ten years older than I was. I had boasted to him about the street girls where I lived. Fortunately, a beautiful girl was in the shop who from her looks and smiles we found out that she was a street girl. She accepted our invitation and came with us to my flat. My friend and I had sex relation with her. She said she had nowhere to stay the night and we were glad to keep her in my flat. After a couple of hours, we went to bed. I did not see her anymore; I guess she had left Sheffield. In another occasion, one of these street girls who had come to my flat told me she had a deaf friend who was a widow. She asked me to go to her house and to be with that woman free! So, she took me to her friend's flat which was not very far away from my flat and introduced me to her. After she left, the woman who was in her thirties started playing with me. She was an ordinary looking woman but was deaf and dumb. I enjoyed having sex relation with her because she pretended was enjoying very much, however, it was a quickie same as usual. I did not use preservative in this occasion either. She looked at me strangely and invited me to go and see her again by waving her hands. After these two occasions, I got a bad rash nearly all over my skin, especially around my genitals. I went to see the University doctor. He was a very kind and a very good doctor. He asked me if I had sex without using preservative. He told me never again have sex without using preservative with street girls. In fact, I had visited him before and had told him I abused myself a lot and wished to leave this bad habit. He had advised me not to do it but had not prescribed a useful way of undoing. He sent me to a clinic. I had to visit the clinic for two weeks every other day. In there I should take a shower, and then a middle-aged man would come and scratch all over my body with a rough skin rubber to get these marks out of my skin. I did not go out with any street girls for a long while until my skin was back to normal.

After the New Year holidays I moved to the University house of lodgings. The hall of residence was an old building which was one time used as a hospital during the Second World War and later as a barrack for soldiers. To the left of the entrance was the dining room. It was a big hall with tables for serving dinner. To the right of the entrance was the reception. There was always at least one person at the reception that checked the students coming in or going out of the hall. Then there were two long corridors one at the left and one at the right side. The right and left wings each consisted of twenty corridors, ten on the left and ten on the right. In each corridor there were ten rooms. So it hosted four hundred students. The right side was designated to male students and the left side to female students. So it was a mixed hall of residence. The boys were not allowed to go to the girls' room after 9 p.m. nor were the girls allowed to go to the boys' room. From 11 p.m. no one was allowed to wonder around even in his corridor. The guards would start walking along the main corridors and checking any student walking around. In case they noticed someone they would remind him to get inside his or her room. No guests were allowed after 8 p.m. and if there was a guest inside he must leave the hall of residence before 9 p.m. In each side of the corridor there was a toilet and a kitchenette with an electric boiler and a sink for washing clothes by hands. The breakfast was served as self-service. Lunch was not served during weekdays. However, the dinner was served during the week days. Tea time started at six p.m. The warden and his colleagues wearing university gowns would enter the dining room and sit on top where they could see everybody. We should wear a gown as well otherwise we were not allowed to get inside the dining room. Also after the warden had arrived and sat down the doors were closed and late comers were not allowed to get inside; they would miss the dinner! So, all students would do their best to get inside the dining room in good time. When the warden arrived all the students would rise and stand up until he was seated. He would then preach some praying and when finished students would say Amen; then the dinner was served by the maids. There was always a kind of soup to start with and then an English dish; roast beef, lamb chops, stew or chicken. The ceremony would last about an hour. No one was allowed to get out of the dining room before the Warden left. I was not used to these formalities but soon got used to it. During weekends all the meals were served as self-service. There were two or three options and we had a choice to choose. For breakfast, there were cereals, orange juice, half of a grapefruit, boiled eggs or fried eggs usually with beans and sausages. I cannot remember other meals but I remember that we enjoyed the dinner very much, especially because we didn't have to stand in long queues. For breakfast and weekend meals there was plenty of time to get the food. Usually at 8 o'clock on week days there was a queue but later it diminished. From January 1967 till end of June when the exams was finished I had a room on the right wing and the first room inside the corridor. I got to know few English boys but I cannot remember their names. One of them was a humorous one and always teased the guards or the maids. I remember he used to ask them if they had got the letter; I didn't understand what he meant but his friends used to laugh a lot when he teased them. The only person I was very friendly with was a student from my country who could not speak my language. He was taken to England at the age of six and he had done all his schooling in England. We used to call him Jim. He was a tall boy darker than me. His parents were from south of my country and rather rich. In summer time he never went home (perhaps because of not being able to speak his mother language), he used his holidays by going abroad usually by tours. His English was perfect with a good accent. He knew a few words of my language but his accent and grammar seemed funny, so he usually kept himself away from my countrymen students. I remember one Tuesday night I knocked on his door and asked if he would like to have a game of chess. He said he studied during weekdays and had fun only during weekends. I returned to my room very unhappy. But now I admire his aspiration for his studies. He was very fun of horse racing and betting. Once we had a bet together on a horse called 'Yellow God' and we won.

In June, I booked a place in hall of residence for the term starting in October. We were supposed to leave the hall of residence in summer. I decided to stay in Sheffield during that summer and not go home. I looked for a flat in an area where students used to live. It was a good area near a beautiful park. There was a student from my country, studying law whom I had met in Student Union. He was a weight lifter and had become champion in student competition several times. His flat was in the next street only five minutes' walk away from the flat I had rented. As I didn't have much to do I slept a lot. I slept in the mornings till 10 o'clock; again in afternoons from 2 to 5 p.m. I only went out for shopping or walking in the park. I watched the girls passing by or sometimes went out looking for street girls. I usually went to their flats since my flat was very far from that area. One day, this new friend knocked on my window, I was asleep. I got up and let him inside my room. He was surprised to see me sleeping at that time of the day. He said he couldn't sleep much and only slept for five or six hours per day. I told him I could sleep any time I decided to sleep. He was surprised to hear that. He urged me to do some exercise and persuaded me to go to the University sport room. I accepted his offer gladly and from the following session I went to the sport room with him. I never forget the first session. He gave me some exercise to warm up and then we ran round the sport hall a few times. Then he showed me weight lifting. He brought small weights; I think I started with ten pounds. He told me to do the exercise ten times. When finished I said it is so easy and I could lift the weights for another ten times. He said you should give it a rest for today, but I did not listen to him and did the exercise for another ten times. As soon as I put down the lifts I got dizzy; it seemed the room was turning around my head, I was pale and lied down on the floor. He said didn't I tell you not to overdo it. I recovered after about ten minutes. He told me not to be put off by this experience and three times a week on Monday, Wednesday and Friday he took me to the sport centre. After four month I noticed that my arms were getting hard, my chest was becoming firm and I was going to get the looks of a sport man. I continued weight lifting with him for about nine months. By that time I could lift 100 pounds. I felt more energetic than ever.

Towards the end of summer vacation one of my friends told me to apply for student grant. Most students from my country had applied for it and used to get it. Fortunately my application for grant was approved and I was going to be paid twelve pounds a week from October 1968 which was a gift for me. I remember I had bought some carrots and left it under wash basin. After a week I noticed it was grown; quite long leaves were coming out from the roots. I did not want to throw them away in a dust bin because I thought they were alive and had the right to live. I bought a couple of vases and went to the nearby Park, and filled the vases with soil. I took the vases home and planted the carrots in them. Also I watered the vases a little bit. To my amazement the carrots grew rapidly and I was very delighted to see them growing. I had a feeling that my looking after the carrots would bring me good luck. In fact it did. First my application for grant was approved and I was admitted to the hall of residence once again. In October 1968 I moved to a new room in the hall of residence. This time my room was at the bottom of a left wing. Opposite to my room were those of female students. Soon I noticed that in the evenings after we had supper in the dining room, the girls came to their room and got undressed and put their home cloths on. To have a better look and be able to peep into their rooms I used to turn the lights off and closed my curtains, then peeping through a small narrow slot left in between the two sides of the curtains. I could peep into three rooms. One of the girls was rather thin and used to wear a head band. She used to take the gown off and usually undressed quickly and then put on a night dress. I enjoyed very much peeping into her room; I used to daydream about her and usually wetted myself when asleep in early mornings. A month had gone; I had bought a gramophone and some records. In the evenings I used to listen to pop music and try to study. I remember a pop record called "those were the days" singed by Mary Hopkins. Beatles had made the music; the song was very romantic and every night I listened to it probably more than ten times. One weekend I was very depressed and sad about my wrong doings. There were so many young and nice girls in the hall of residence, most of them had boyfriends, English of course but I had not any girlfriends. It was a Sunday, I had got up late and I had missed the breakfast. I had abused myself the night before; perhaps I had dreamed a lot. I tried to go for lunch as soon as possible. I dressed up and went to the dining room. There were two girls in front of me. Some students were coming to get lunch lazily. It appeared all those who were coming early for lunch had missed the breakfast. When I got my tray, I followed the two girls and asked them if I could sit with them on the same table. One of them smiled and said I could. I had my lunch with them. The girl who was prettier had a boyfriend, talked about her boyfriend, and left soon. The other girl called Lidia kept on talking. When I told her I was reading Mechanical Engineering and that I was in the third year she was so delighted to hear that because she was first year student also reading Mechanical Engineering. We talked a lot about the lecturers and the laboratories. She also wanted to know where I was from. We had talked for about two hours! They were going to close the dining room. So we left the dining room, on the way to our rooms she asked me if I wanted a cup of tea; I said yes. Then I told her I would go to my room and put the kettle on. She said she would go to her room and would return in half an hour. For the first time in my life a young girl had in fact made a pass on me and was going to come to my room. I went to my room first, put the kettle on in the kitchenette, which was located in the beginning of the wing. My room was at the end of the wing. Then I rushed to my room tiding up. I had some photos of nude models taken out from Playboy magazines on the wall of my room next to my bed. I decided to take them off from the wall before she arrives. However, while I was trying to get them off she knocked on my door and came in. She had come sooner than she had said. I was embarrassed, but she told me with a smile not to worry. She said she knew all boys liked these photos and why I wanted to hide them from her. Anyway tea got ready soon and I poured two cups of tea. I turned on my gramophone and played some records for her. She told me she wasn't really fun of pop music but liked Jazz music very much. She stayed with me until we went for supper together. She came to my room again to listen to music. In the meantime we talked a lot about our families; studies and interests. She stayed until half past nine then she said "oh dear I cannot go to my room this time of the night because the guards are on their duty now". She asked me if she could stay the night in my room and I was so delighted to hear that. All my dreams were coming true. She said she would go to her room early morning. There was a single bed in all the rooms, and before eleven o'clock, we went to bed together. Of course she hadn't brought her night dress and she didn't take off her clothes. She was wearing a blouse and a skirt. I slept next to her and held her in my arms till morning. Later I started kissing her and robbed her breasts. She told me off and said it was too soon. She said we didn't know each other and it was better to wait until we get to know each other more. I didn't insist first of all because I had abused myself the night before and secondly I thought now that she has come to my room I better behave like a gentleman not like a hungry dog. The next morning we went for the breakfast together and then took the bus together. I was feeling very proud and very happy indeed. After living five years in England, I was having a girlfriend. We were almost together all the time for the next three days. She went to her room on Monday and Tuesday night. But on Wednesday night she stayed in my room till late. She slept with me and we had intimate relation in the midnight, but I was so excited that I had a premature ejaculation. I apologized for that but she told me not to worry. She said it was because of getting too excited. I knew it was because of over self- abusing. However, two nights later had a successful love making. She had given me confidence and that was what I needed. She was rather shy and did not like me to look at her body. However in bed she hardly refused me. I liked her attitude towards sex relation and enjoyed myself very much while being with her.

Two weeks later, I received a letter from my schoolmate who was my boyfriend back home. I was very surprised to hear from him after so many years. He said in his letter that he had a grant from the army to read for Mechanical Engineering. He was doing 'A' levels in a college in London. He had invited me to go and see him in London. I told Lidia that I had heard from this schoolmate and I could not wait to go and see him. Therefore, I went to London to see my old boyfriend. He was living with some other students from my country. He said they were paid quite a lot because working in the army was regarded as a hardship. He said he had a girlfriend and boasted about her. He said all his friends had found girlfriends in that short period they had come to London and that had sex relation more or less every night. I told him I had a girlfriend as well. He said he would like to see her and I told him on my next visit to London I would take her with me. On my return to Sheffield, I had brought a few presents for Lidia. Couple of creams, lipsticks and nail varnish. She was surprised and told me only one of them would have been enough. I had missed her a lot but on my return I didn't invite her until Wednesday. She came to my room with tears and said why I had got so cold with her. I told her I had fallen in love with her and I thought it would be better to break our relation before we get deeply involved. She said she loved me as well and did not want me to break up with her. I held her in my arms and kissed her a lot. Then we went to bed together. I never forget that moment because it was very memorable.

After a few weeks of getting each other better known, we had sex relation almost every night. One evening, when we were getting back from the dining room she suddenly fell on the ground and was screaming from a harsh pain in her knees. I held her up and asked the guard to call an ambulance. I went with her to the hospital. While in the ambulance I was holding her hands in my hands and told her not to worry. I told her she would recover soon and I kissed her on her cheeks. I told her I loved her and would accompany her in her misery and happiness; in her pains and sorrows. We passed each other our love feelings. I remember the ambulance driver had seen us kissing each other in the mirror and was telling the man next to him that look they even don't care even in the ambulance while she is bearing pain. The other man said they are young and it is their right to love each other. Any way I accompanied her all the time in Emergency section of the hospital. The physician gave her some creams to use to relieve the pain and told her she must have a ligament operation on her knees. He said it has a killing pain when it shows itself and then registered her name for the operation. He said he would notify her as soon as they had a vacancy for the operation. In the British system students were on National Health Service and all their medical expenses were free of charge. Even big and costly operations were free but usually one had to wait for a long time. Later she told me a brief story of her life. She said she was born after her parents had lost their first child, which was a son. She said her father always wanted a son and when she was born, her father treated her as a boy and replaced her by his late son in his mind. She said, as her father was an mechanical engineer encouraged her to read Mechanical Engineering as well. She had a sister who was two years younger than she was. Later her sister came to visit her in Sheffield. I cannot remember her name but her sister was much more beautiful than she was. In my view Lidia was not pretty at all; she was an ordinary girl. When she became my girlfriend, she was only 18 years old. I was not a handsome boy either; to my view my body physic was ordinary as well. So, we matched together all right.

Gradually all my friends and her friends knew that we were having close relations. We were almost together all the time except at lecture times because we had different courses. We had our breakfast together and had lunch together on the same table at University. Studied together in the library and went home together. Towards the end of December, we were told that we had to move to newly built house of residence near the University Campus and near the football ground. In January 1969 we moved to the new hall of residence. It was a modern building. Eight stories all together. The first four stories were designated to male students and the next four stories were designated to female students. My room was on the ground floor and Lidia's room was on the eighth floor. The rules were relaxed. There were no more dinner ceremonies with the Guardian; no need to wear gown at dinnertime and to our surprise the time limit for girls staying at boys' rooms or vice versa was relaxed to midnight. My life in this hall of residence was very good. Lidia did not let me to bet on horses any more. She encouraged me to save my money and spend extras on other things like going to London or having dinner at a restaurant. I remember one winter evening perhaps in February we went to a posh restaurant. We went by bus and walked for few minutes from the bus station to the restaurant. We both wore glasses and when we entered the restaurant our faces was nearly frozen. The restaurant was very warm inside and as soon as we entered, our glasses were steamed so much that we hardly could see anywhere! A man came towards us and guided us towards a table. We sat there and took off our overcoats. We noticed that the restaurant was crowded and almost everybody there were looking at us. Lidia told me not to worry and not to care. Perhaps as we entered we couldn't find our way to a table, because the room was dark and warm and our glasses were steamed. We ordered steak and talked to each other. On the way back we took a bus and by the time we got home it was about eleven.

Our relation with each other got closer and closer. She used to come to my room in the evenings after tea time and stay the night with me. We didn't quarrel on anything. Only once she played a jazz record for an hour or so; I took it off from the gramophone and played a pop music by Rolling Stones. After half an hour she said she didn't want to hear it any more. I told her if she doesn't like it she better leave my room. She left my room and didn't come to my room for two days. I went to her room on the eighth floor, apologized for my behaviour and stayed the night in her room for the first time. That was the only time I was rude to her. I remember one Saturday afternoon; I was walking along the road to the University thinking how happy I now was after living alone so many years in England. I remember I wore a new suit, which was greenish, having smile on my face because I was better off than previous years enjoying twelve pounds a week grant on top of money I received from home. I was proud having a girlfriend and more over I was quite satisfied enjoying intimate relation whenever I desired. She never refused me. Sometimes we made love in the afternoon; then once more when we went to bed and again in early morning. If it was Sunday, we had it again before lunch, after lunch and so on. She decided to go home for the new years' holidays. I went to the train station with her and kissed her on her cheeks as she left. I told her I would miss her. She stayed home for two weeks. In March 1969 once, I went to her room. I had noticed she was upset for the last few days but did not mention why. This time I asked her why she looked so miserable; she said she had missed her period for a week and she thought she was pregnant. I told her not to worry. I told her if she were pregnant, it would be our child and I would marry her. I was honest in my sayings, because I believed that if she was pregnant it would be our child and I should not leave her with an unwanted child. I told her I would write a letter home and tell my parents that I have a girlfriend and want to marry her. She smiled at me, held me in her arms, and told me she was relieved a great deal. She said it was on her mind for the last few days and did not dare to tell me about it. Indeed, as soon as I got to my room I wrote a letter to my father and told him that I had found a girlfriend and I thought we were in love with each other and finally that I wanted to marry her. It usually took about a month before I received a reply from home. Few days after this meeting she came to my room with a smile and said that she had her period back and there was no need to worry about having a child. She said she didn't want to be pregnant while she was studying. Going to classes with a big tommy she said! I was glad to hear that as well. How could I tell my parents that I had a child? In my journeys home, my father always boasted to others that my son does not smoke, does not drink and does not have a girlfriend. He was right. I did not drink alcohol; I smoked for a while but soon I had given it up. I didn't want to hide it from my father, so one summer when I went home I gave it up for good. I did not have a girlfriend for five years!

I think it was in early April when we went to visit London together. My schoolmate had invited us to go to London. He insisted I take Lidia with me. So we arranged to visit him during a weekend. It was her first journey to London. My schoolmate took us around and showed us several places and we took many photographs. We went to Piccadilly Circus, Hyde Park and London Museum. These were all very interesting for Lidia. For bedtime, we stayed in his room. Lidia and I slept in his bed and he and his girlfriend slept on the floor. He wanted to show me he had a steady girlfriend as well. I think he did not believe that I had a girlfriend and wanted to see if I was right. To him I was a shy boy who couldn't make a pass to girls. I also wanted to show him that I was not a lonely boy any more being pleased by talking to handsome boys. I was very proud to have Lidia with me, to me it seemed as if I had all the world at my hand I was feeling very happy and proud of myself. While sleeping I whispered to Lidia and asked for love making. She was very reluctant but even then in the darkness of the room and quietness we made love. I wanted to prove to my schoolmate that I could and I think by the squeaks of the bed he and his girlfriend noticed that we were making love to each other. Soon after that we fell asleep and I don't know if he and his girlfriend made love to each other or not. I am sure they did as well.

After a month, I received a letter from my father regarding marrying Lidia. He said he really did not mind but wanted to know what we would call our baby. What would be his religion? What would be his language? He also mentioned that girls from my hometown were more faithful to their husbands. He said in his letter that since I was twelve years old my name was fixed to my mothers' cousin named Sara. She was now eighteen years old only, five years younger than I was, in the last year of high school and I must make my mind. If I did not want to marry her, I must let them know soon. He asked me in his letter to think for a while and not decide in a rush. When I read his letter I was shocked and thought I better think about what he had written. I thought if a foreign girl loves me so much a hometown girl would love me much more! Other points he had brought up was also right. My child would have a mixed culture. I then started telling Lidia that my marriage depends on my parents. I must get their permission. She told me my beloved friend I would do whatever you tell me and would go anywhere you tell me. I told her if you come to my hometown, you must wear hijab (scarf), you must change your religion and learn to speak our language. She said she didn't mind and would do them no matter what. I told her it is too hot in my hometown in summer time and she cannot tolerate that heat. She said even if I told her to go to the hell she would go; she would come with me and would never let me alone she said. Now that I think about her feelings I can see she was really in love with me but I was not! I told her there is my mother's cousin waiting for me to go back and marry her but I will try to satisfy my parents to get married with you. She looked at me strangely but did not comment.

For Easter holidays, she invited me to go to her parent's house with her. I accepted and received a warm welcome from her father. Her father was working with a famous factory. He showed me some of his inventions and told me he would take me to the factory in summer where his daughter and I could work as beginners. Lidia's mother was somehow reluctant to accept me as her daughter's boyfriend. Lidia showed me the beautiful sceneries of their village. Their home was on top of a hill whose name I cannot remember. I slept in a separate room and was their guest for three days. I think her father had accepted me as his son-in-law but her mother did not.

In May 1969 just before the exams started, she got a letter from the hospital that they had given her time for ligament operation. She informed her supervisor and asked her mum to come over. She didn't turn up only her sister came to Sheffield and stayed for a couple of days. I accompanied her to the hospital and after the operation I was the first person to meet her in the hospital. I went to her bedside held her hands in my arms and told her I loved her. There were tears in my eyes seeing her so pale and having pain. She said she would be alright and would come home soon. It was 10 O'clock on a Wednesday morning that she was brought to the house of residence by an ambulance. The woman warden of the house saw me holding her hands and taking her to the lift to her room. When in her room she lied down in her bed and I started kissing her and telling her how much I missed her. Then she locked her door and I got off my clothes and went to bed with her. We were just having intimate relation that suddenly we heard someone knocking on her door. It was the lady warden. She screamed 'Open the door'. I whispered let me get up and put on my clothes and open the door, but she said no just remain still. Suddenly the door was opened. Of course she had the master key of all the rooms. There was her supervisor as well. As they entered the room they saw us sleeping together. They said 'Oh dear' and left the room. We got off quickly and put on our clothes on. We went downstairs and I went to my room. She said she would go to see the warden. She told me she had said why they had opened her room without her permission and the warden had said we should either get married or stop our relations. The next day I received a letter from the University Physician. He wanted to see me and talk to me urgently. On my visit to him, he told me that we should be careful, use preservatives and be aware of skin diseases. He knew me quite well. I told him I intended to marry Lidia and I did not worry if she gets pregnant. He then told me to be careful in front of other students! After this event, rumours were spread that Lidia and I were engaged and were going to get married. I had taken an extra course in mathematics and wanted to read for the degree of MSc in applied mathematics. I remember in 1968 before finding Lidia, once I was having lunch in the student union of the university, there was a lecturer from The Big City near my hometown University doing his sabbatical leave in Medical department. He asked me what I intended to do after graduation. I told him I become a mechanical engineer and intend to work as an engineer in a steel plant. He laughed at me and said why in a steel mill. He said it would be a tough job and since I was a quiet and soft person, he did not recommend me doing that. Instead, he said it would be better if you obtain your MSc degree and apply to teach in a university. That's why I decided to continue my studies. As I have mentioned before, my grades in mathematics were excellent and my supervisor had made the suggestion to do MSc in applied mathematics. I had informed my father that I intended to continue my studies and he had accepted it. Any way after the exams, I went to the Mathematics Department and was interviewed by the head of the department. He told me I could read for the Master's degree in his department although my BSc was an ordinary degree.

I sat for my exams in June and passed all the subjects this time. I was granted the BSc degree in Mechanical Engineering (an ordinary degree; in England they didn't give the average marks but the levels were honorary degree for the highest grades, general degree for the average grades and ordinary degree for those who had just passed). Lidia only sat for some of her subjects. Her operation was in the middle of her exams. I told her not to worry and said I would help her more in the next academic year. I had planned to go home for summer holidays to see if I could get my parents approval of getting married with Lidia. Inside me, there was turmoil. If Lidia loves me so much certainly, Sara would love me much more. I had noticed that once Lidia took me to her room, some of her neighbour friends had come to visit her after her operation. When she went to serve tea I noticed most of her friends showed a kind of affection towards me as if they wanted me to become their boyfriend as if they wanted me to go and make love to them. I don't know what Lidia had told them; maybe she had said I was a hot boy and had sex relation with her every night. May be she had exaggerated as we used to do when talking about our girlfriends. Remember my weight lifter friend had told me he had made love to his girlfriend six times in one night. I always thought he could have done that because he was a weight lifter and a strong man. He had said his love making lasted more than half an hour each time. My love making with Lidia was always less than ten minutes. About four or five minutes was foreplay; getting her ready. As soon as I was aroused I would have sex relation and it lasted a minute or two at the most. She never blamed me for coming so quickly or not having enjoyed fully. She was rather shy as well; we never had oral sex together and she never let me look at her vagina. She always looked satisfied with me and never put me off or said any words letting me down. I remember one of her friends was from Northern Ireland and had a special accent. She tried to attract me more than her other friends and asked me to see her again. This event made me confident that finally I was in the middle of attention in girl's talks and that I was a hot pot as one of London prostitutes had told me a few years back. I was thinking that with my experience of lovemaking, Sara would love me much more than Lidia and especially as she was not with any other man, she would appreciate my lovemaking and do so and so for me. I would have an excellent married life. Some other times I thought Lidia was very honest and kind. I had spent the most enjoyable and memorable time of my life with her and why should I let her go and break her heart. I couldn't make my mind. I told myself I would go to my hometown and see what happens.

The day of parting arrived. Lidia had to go to her hometown and stay with her parents until next October when the new term would start. I had booked my tickets and would be going home soon. She gave me a small suitcase containing her books and clothes and I left it in the weightlifter's house with my own luggage. I was told that I had to find a new place for accommodation in October. My weightlifter friend was a kind friend and accepted to keep our luggage until I found a new place for living in October.

It was two O'clock on a Friday afternoon when I went to the bus station with Lidia. I kissed her and said good bye to her and when the bus started moving she stood up and waved her hands to me. I had sat down and was crying. She could see tears coming down my cheeks so she sat down quickly. The bus accelerated and I couldn't see her face any more. I am sure she cried as well when the bus left. I don't know why I was crying. Perhaps I was crying because I had a feeling that I may not see her again. Perhaps I was crying because I loved her and missed her a lot. I had a mixed feeling. I left for London a few days later and flied home after a week. Before leaving England I wrote her a love letter and said how much I missed her and that I was hopeful to get my parent's approval for marrying her. In The Capital I was in my grandfather's house and I showed her photos to my family in The Capital.

CHAPTER 4

I-4 Getting married

Back in my hometown, I received a warm welcome from my family. We soon went to the village and one evening went to Sara's house to visit her. My mother was with me too. They seemed to be happy seeing us there. Sara asked a few questions about my studies. She said she had obtained her diploma and intended to continue her studies. Her brother was studying in Germany and said she would like to go abroad for studying. All the time I looked at her carefully. She was a beautiful girl much more beautiful than Lidia was. She was nineteen rather tall and thin with full firm breasts. Her body physics was like fashion models very sexy looking. I loved her smiles and the way she talked to me. I knew her since she was born. I remember when she was born in January 1950 we were invited to their house. There her father who was my mother's relative said to my mum that I would like to give you my daughter to be your bride for your son. Afterwards when she was growing up I had a special eye on her. As she grew up, her father always reminded my mother that Sara was for me. Her mother also approved it. Especially, Sara had a brother who was very keen to marry my second sister and our parents had agreed that Sara would be for me and my sister would be for her brother. An arranged marriage would take place if everything went according as planned. In my talks with Sara, I did not notice any reluctance; I thought she looked happy seeing me. Back at home my mother asked my opinion about marrying her. I told her how I could tell Lidia about it. I actually had changed my mind and wanted to marry Sara instead. I was thinking to myself that she was much prettier than Lidia; besides she was a virgin girl from our own family. Although her father had passed away, but her mother was very keen on me.

My father also asked my opinion about Sara and I told him without hesitation that she was ideal for me and I would rather marry her than marrying my English girlfriend. He was glad to hear that. I decided to write a letter to Lidia and tell her the story systematically. In my first letter I said I was missing her a lot but regarding our marriage my parents had chosen a girl who is our relative and I had known her from my childhood. I told her our customs here is different with theirs in England but I was going to work on them and was trying my best to see what I could do. After three weeks I received her reply. She said in her letter that I was fooling her and she wanted me to tell her the truth; weather I really loved her and if I really wanted her. By this time, my father had gone to Sara's house and talked to her mother. He had said our proposal is for Sara and regarding my sister for her brother, they better ask him and inform us. My father had said that he was not in a good financial situation and suggested that Sara and I get married after my studies, which would take only one year. Her mother had said she was very pleased to hear that but it would be a great idea if Sara could get married right away and come with me to England it would be ideal for them. My father had said that the cost of studying in England was very high and he was not in a financial situation to pay for living and education expenses of both of us. Later my father told my mother and me what he had done and their response to his proposal. I wrote a letter to Lidia immediately and made an excuse telling her due to the pressure I was going to get married with my mother's cousin and it was an arranged marriage. I asked her to forgive me for breaking her heart. Just before returning to England I received a letter from her saying that she was really broken hearted and even if she forgives me there is God punishment as consequences which meant I would get broken hearted in future by someone else. I didn't like reading her letter any more. She had said she did not go out of her home for two weeks and was crying all the time feeling really broken hearted. However, one of her friends had told her not to worry; the world is full of men and soon she would find somebody else to love. Now regarding my marriage, my father told me I had to wait for another year until I finish my studies. I told him I wanted to get married now because I was afraid she might get married by next year to someone else. He said there is no point to worry. Even if she gets married, he said there are plenty of girls in our hometown that I can go and make a proposal for you. He was so sure of himself that said anybody you choose would be glad to get married with you. In response, I told him that I only wanted to marry Sara; otherwise, I would marry Lidia. When I came to The Capital to fly to London, I stayed in my grandfather's house for a few days. I wrote a letter to Sara in it I said how much I loved her and that her thought was all the time in my mind. My mother noticed the letter in my hands, grabbed it from me, and started reading it eagerly. I must admit that she is a very nosey person!

Back in England, as soon as I got to Sheffield I looked for a bedsitter. I found a room in a house, which accommodated some other foreign students from Nigeria and Turkey. When settled in this flat and did my registration as a MSc student in Mathematics Department, I started chasing street girls once again. I used to buy porn magazines, reading the stories getting excited and then either I abused myself or if I had a bit of money went to the street in which sluts wondered around.

I met Lidia one day in dining room of the Student Union where most students had their lunch there. She told me she wanted to come and get her luggage from me. I gave her the address and asked her to come to my flat next day (which was Saturday) about 10'o'clock. She arrived just on time and as soon as I gave her luggage she wanted to leave. She was very upset with me and didn't want to look at me never mind to talk to me. I grabbed her hands and pushed her on the bed and while apologizing for what had happened I asked her to make love just one more time. Although she was reluctant and did not appreciate it at all, however, she let me make love to her. She then left and wished happiness for me. I saw her one more time about six months later walking with a coloured boy whom I think was her new boyfriend. I never saw her again.

After a month I received a letter from Sara that it was her ambition to come to England to be with me and to study English. I wrote a letter to my father and said if Sara does not come to England then I cannot concentrate on my studies. Poor man had gone to Sara's mother and said, "I can send Sara to England but I cannot ask my son to come over for wedding ceremonies. If you agree I send my son a deputation letter by which we can wed the bride and send her over to England". They accepted his offer and my father sent me a letter telling me to send him deputation letter. I went to our Embassy in London, obtained the letter, and posted it. Meanwhile I was going out with the street girls more or less every night. Although I knew I should behave myself because I was going to sleep with a virgin girl but somehow my eager for street girls had increased, I thought it was my last chance to go out with street girls. I attended all my classes on time and tried to do all the exercises but in my spare time I was either in betting office or looking for street girls. Before chasing a street girl, I was so excited and imagined all kind of sex positions but as soon as it was over, I did not want to look at them or even talk to them. I wanted them to leave me alone so that I could sleep. I would fall sleep very quickly and my emotions was calm for a day or two. In that short period, I could concentrate on my studies. When frustrated again I spent a lot of time studying horses records. I used to bet a lot, which usually ended in losing money and wasting my precious time as well. Just before Christmas holidays I received a letter from my father that my second sister was getting married to my cousin. He was nineteen and my sister was seventeen. In summer there was rumours that my sister had fallen in love with him but getting married was out of imagination, because my father had mentioned many times that he was not in a good financial situation at all. So hearing that surprised me a lot. He wrote he had talked to Sara's mother and told her I could go home during these holidays and marry her at the same time. I wanted to marry her as soon as possible but I did not like the idea of two marriage ceremonies at the same time. My father sent fifty pounds for my travel expenses and buying gifts. It was not much. I soon booked a one-month return ticket and rented an apartment so that when I returned from home I could take my wife there without hesitation. I went to London, bought a beautiful pink cashmere blouse for eight pounds from the free shop in the airport for her, and flew home. I went to my hometown straight away. Our wedding ceremony was supposed to take place in ten days' time in January 1970. First news was that Sara's brother had come from Germany and he wanted our ceremony to take place separately. Well my parents agreed to postpone my sister's wedding for a week. One evening I wanted to go to Sara's house saying hello to her and give her my present but as soon as I took that pink blouse out of my suitcase, my sister grabbed it from me and asked me to give it to her. I said I had brought it for my fiancé but she said she was a new bride and wanted that too. I didn't resist at all and gave it to her. Later I was very sorry for that because Sara and her mother blamed me many times that the new groom came to our house empty handed. The week before our wedding was rather unpleasant because Sara's mother had changed her attitude towards us all together. They sent a message and said they wanted to ask our opinion about designing the wedding card and to see how many people to invite. My father was very reluctant to go and had told them it didn't matter for him and they could do what they wanted to do. But on their persistence we went to their house. We were lead to their guest room. To our surprise, they were some unexpected guests; Sara's grandfather, uncle, brother in law and her mother who brought in some tea and sweets for us. Grandfather started speaking. He said that he was very pleased for this wedding, but he wanted my father to do his best for this wedding. He then asked to pay fifty thousand dollars (equivalent to 3000 gold coins) as her Dowry, a kind of wedding guarantee (this money should be paid to the bride in case she wants to get divorce or when there is a quarrel between them). My father got annoyed when he heard that; he said he had discussed this matter with her mother and she had accepted his suggestion. My father got up angrily and told me let us go. I got up and followed him. In the corridor, I saw my fiancé crying in the next room. I went inside to calm her down. Instead, she cried loudly and said to her mother she did not want to marry me; "let him go" she said and told me to leave her and not to touch her. I was very surprised to see that and left their house without saying anything. I followed my father but I didn't tell him what I had heard and seen. Back at home, he told me to go back to England and forget about the marriage. I didn't say anything but in the following morning I told him how could I get back while I had told my friends I would return with a wife and I had rented a flat for it. He said he reckons they want our money and they have changed so much from summer up to now. I guess my father was right but he did not want to accept that his doings was wrong as well. Firstly he wanted the marriage to take place after I finished my studies, secondly he wanted the ceremony to be held by deputation and lastly he wanted joint ceremony with my sister's wedding. In addition, my mother had said that we had guests from other cities and so they should keep the groom just after ceremony for the wedding night. I hadn't brought a gift for the bride and had not told my parents to pay special attention to them. Also my sister was marrying her own cousin and had not waited for their son. After two days Sara's uncle came to see my father and said you have invited your family from other cities and invited guests for the wedding; your son has come from England and everybody is talking about this wedding. He asked why he got angry and it would be better to let the ceremony to take place. He said he had also talked to the bride's family and had obtained their consent for the wedding. I was pleased to hear that but somehow I was not happy at all. I had a feeling that there was something wrong somehow and had mixed feelings. On the other hand my sister was feeling very happy for her wedding and wished it happened sooner. Her fiancé was also happy and my parents had concentrated all their attention to her wedding but not me. Thus, our wedding ceremony was arranged. On a Thursday night, in January we went to their house. About hundred guests were invited; including my grandparents and aunts. The atmosphere was very cool. The men were sitting in a room at left side of the house and the women at the right side. A woman was singing wedding songs. The audience were clapping and young girls aged eight to fourteen were dancing. After the mullahs obtained our permission for marriage from us and our parents, they brought in the wedding documents to be signed. We were officially married! I was then asked to go and see the bride and take some photographs with her and her family. Her mother had asked me to invite a photographer and I had asked an old photographer to come. On this important day he had got ill and had sent over his young son to take photographs. I don't know what he did but later the photographer apologized for ruining all the photographs by his son. He even didn't give us a single photograph. He said his son had opened the camera and all the slides were blackened! Did this mean that our wedding was going to be ruined same as the photographs? I had a bad feeling about this event. I was taken to the wedding room. Sara was wearing a white wedding dress and standing next to her brother. It appeared as if her brother was the groom not me! She didn't even look at me, was very solemn looking not happy at all. She pretended to my mother and sisters as if she was happy and took some photographs with all of us. Later they brought some meal for us. But before that I felt stomach problem, diarrhoea. I went to toilet a few times and no one asked how I was. I ate the meal with her very reluctantly. About 10 o'clock all the guests had gone home. I was left alone. They had some guests; her aunts and cousins and her brother. I was told to stay the night to sleep with her and take her virginity off. I wasn't in a good mood at all. At bedtime, her mother came to me and said our house is full of guests and you had better go to your own home; we cannot have you here tonight, she said. I heard the bride crying to her mum that she had a headache and did not want to see me. She was saying in a loud voice "send him home!" So, I walked home in that winter night. Our house was not too far away from their house, but it took me about half an hour to walk to get home. Back home my mother asked me why they didn't keep me for the night and I said they had too many guests and could not keep me. I did not tell her that Sara had shouted loudly. The next day I went to their house about 10 o'clock in the morning. They lead me to a room with Sara but she let her cousins to come to the room. One of them was a fourteen-year-old girl who kept talking all the time to Sara. I was supposed to be let alone with her but she was very reluctant to talk to me. I went home for lunch and returned to their house in the evening. Again, her mother said you better go home and sleep in your own house. For three nights I was sent home. When my father noticed that he told me it is better I go to England without her. I said how could I do that? I had told all my friends that I was going home to get married and bring my wife over; especially to my supervisor that I might be rather late for my classes. I think the rumour that I was returning to England without her had spread. On Sunday morning when I went to see Sara she smiled at me, brought tea with sweets and asked me to stay for lunch. Then she took me to her room and locked it from inside. She was wearing a beautiful purple dress. She had some cosmetics on and looked very beautiful. I felt happy for a moment and tried to kiss her. Although she refused at first but she let me kiss her. Then I slept next to her on the carpet and started to kiss her all over her face. I grabbed her breasts and tried to take off her clothes. Although she was resisting but soon I got her breasts out of her bra. Her body was the most beautiful body I had ever seen. Her figure was very slim, white and firm. We both were getting excited breathing hard. I was ready to make love to her that suddenly her brother knocked on the door. He was saying please open the door, "I want to take out something I had left" and then started shouting. All our feelings were let down. We put on our clothes and I asked Sara to open the door for him and see what he wanted. She whispered not to bother and let's continue kissing. Soon her mother came to the door and told Sara to open the door. She opened the door and we went out to the next room. Her brother had left the house angrily. I said good bye and went home. I didn't stay for the lunch. Sara's mother came to the door and said you must stay here tonight. In the evening I went to their house again. Sara did not welcome me as I was expecting; however, after dinner they guided us to a bedroom. The room was cold in that winter night. There was a paraffin heater in the room. The bed was spread on the carpet and two heavy blankets were provided. As we lied down in the bed we went under the blankets and tried to get warm in that freezing room. I soon started kissing her but she did not respond as in the morning. Then I tried to hold her tight and to say love verses. She resisted a lot and started shouting, "let me go! Don't touch me and so on". Therefore, I let her go and both of us fall asleep soon. In the morning, her mother was quite kind to me and brought in a tray of breakfast. She also brought in a gold watch and a gold ring. Sara was quite kind. Her mother whispered something to her. I guess she had asked her about our bedtime. They kept me for lunch and told me to come back in the evening. When I came to their house in the evening, I noticed the house was rather empty. Sara's brother had left for Germany. All her cousins and aunts had gone home. There were, Sara, me her mother and two old women; apparently their relatives who I had never seen before. One of them was saying bring something for our groom to weave! Later I understood what she meant; she was implying that since the groom had not deflower the bride, so he must do weaving like what old women used to do in my country! Any way I had decided to do my best that night even if she refused me, I would do my best to deflower her virginity! At home, I was urged to show my manhood and return home proudly. When we went to the same bedroom, I noticed that her mother and their guests had left the house and we were left in the house on our own. As soon as we lay down in the bed, I started kissing her and tried to pull off her nightdress. I think I started too soon, because she was not in the right mood at all. I had decided to show my manhood by force. I tried very hard to make love to her. She was shouting loudly and forcing me to get away from her. In this attempt before penetrating her, I had a premature ejaculation. She was wet. She was very annoyed and cleaned herself. Then she leaned over to the wall and started crying and saying that "You are not strong enough! You are not a man! You are damn ugly and I do not love you at all….", and things like that. I remembered my first night with Lidia. I was not able to make love to her but she said it was natural and told me not to worry. Here Sara was quite acting conversely. She was saying she was unhappy because I failed making love to her. I told her not to worry and said I would be successful in my next attempt. It was a very bad night for me. After an hour or so, we fell asleep. In the morning, I did not know how to look at her and her mother. After breakfast, I wanted to get out from their house as soon as I could. I heard Sara was crying and telling her mother she did not want me. Her mother was telling her not to worry. It has been his first attempt, soon he will be okay, she said. I went home. There, I was questioned about our bedtime. I did not have anything to say. I looked very anxious and worried. I should go to The Capital as soon as I could to get passport for her. I was told to go and stay another night with her. That night was unsuccessful as well. Again, I had a premature ejaculation. She sat next to the bed and cried all night. I told her I had been with girls before and there is no point to get worried. This would be okay soon. She fell asleep about 4 a.m. In the morning at breakfast, she was crying again but her mother was telling her not to worry. I was very ashamed and did not know what to say or what to do. My sister's wedding was supposed to be on Thursday; however as she did not want to be present for my sister's wedding she agreed to come to The Capital with me. Bus tickets were bought for Sara, my eldest sister's husband and me. The bus left the station at 8 p.m. It was supposed to arrive in The Capital at 6 a.m. The bus was an old bus and as soon as it left my hometown, lots of dust entered the bus. Sara was leaning on me but soon my stomach was upset. In fact, I vomited twice during the journey. It was a very cold night and since the road to The Capital was not asphalted as it is now, lots of dust got inside the bus. I remember I was trembling from the cold weather and every two or three hours had to ask the driver to stop for a while so that I could vomit. What a terrible night it was. Finally, the bus got to The Capital about 11 a.m. There was my grandfather's chauffer waiting for us. He took us to my grandfather's house and my grandfather who had returned from my hometown and had not stayed for my sister's wedding welcomed us. A room was devoted for us, they wanted us to be alone. Fortunately, Sara got her period and I felt relieved for a few days. The next day I applied for her passport and fortunately, we got it in a week's time. We could not phone directly to my hometown yet so we had to write letters but Sara and I did not have anything to write about to our families. After she got her passport, we booked our tickets to fly back to London and soon we left. During these days, her behaviour with me was friendly. She did not cry any more nor did she blame me for my weakness in making love to her. We arrived in London about 8 p.m. and went to a cheap hotel near Victoria Station. By the time, we got to the hotel it was about 10 p.m. and soon we went to bed because we had a tiring day. After half an hour or so I held Sara closely and tried to make love to her. She threw me away, said she was very tired. The next day we went to Sheffield and went to the flat I had rented. It was a two-storey house. The owner was living downstairs and they had let the top floor to us. The owner was a married couple with two children in his thirties. He and his wife were very pleasant and were glad to have let their house to a newlywed couple. After a few days' rest, I tried to make love to her, but I again I was not successful although I had tried hard, every time, I had a premature ejaculation. My worries were accumulating now. I thought excessive self- abusing and having excessive sex with street girls just before marriage had caused such a weakness. In addition, Lidia's spell on me (perhaps) was another reason for all this. Two months passed. My sorrows were increasing. I was very frustrated. My studies were a problem as well. I had to choose a subject for my dissertation. However, I used to leave the house quickly and go to the university. There were three of us doing MSc with me; a boy from Siam, an English boy and me. I cannot remember their names but I used to copy my homework off the English boy. The Siamese friend was a shy and quiet person like me. Sara's anxiety was increasing and she wrote to her mother that she was still virgin and asked if she could get divorced! By hearing that, I went to see the university physician. He knew about my problems. Once I had told him that I had the bad habit of abusing myself and he only had advised me not to do it excessively. Another time I consulted him for the rash I had from that street girls and last time was about my relationship with Lidia. He was surprised to hear that I had not married Lidia but instead I had married with a girl from my country. He said he must examine my wife. I told Sara that the university doctor must examine her. First, she refused and said she was quite healthy and blamed me for weakness, but as I insisted, she came with me to see the University physician. After examination, he told me that her hymen is very thick and so he had punctured it by a needle. He gave me some cream to use in the night and told me to be gentle with her. That night I did as he had said. Finally, success achieved after two months! Soon after, our bed was full of blood. She was nearly bleeding all night and moaning from the pain. I told her it was not my fault; it was due to her own hymen that was a rare case. In the morning, she was exhausted and fell fast asleep. Later I visited University physician and told him about the problem. He said she had a thick hymen and must have had lots of pain and bleeding. He said this is a rare case and you have been very unfortunate to come across with this problem. I was rather relieved to hear this but I thought all these events were because I had broken Lidia's heart. Sometimes I thought of the good times I had with Lidia and now since the first day of my wedding with Sara I never had a good time at all. After a week or so, I made love to her but each time I had a premature ejaculation.

Now she was no longer a virgin but she never got satisfied from bedtime relation. Again, she started blaming me for being week. I was wondering what was wrong with me. I went to a cinema one day on my own and watched a porn film. I was excited most of the time and when coming home fancied having sex with a street girl but I did not. At home, I tried to make love to my wife but I did not know why I was not so successful. My experience with Lidia was the same but she never blamed me. Even if she was not satisfied, she never brought it to my face as we say; however, now with my wife who was much more beautiful than Lidia was and much sexier than her I could not get her satisfaction for even once. To me she was a perfect woman, an ideal partner for any tastes.

I had some friends from my country in Sheffield; two of them were married and had two children. They were older than I was. We arranged to meet each other at weekends and this helped a lot for Sara not to feel very lonely. Three days a week she used to go to an old English woman's house to learn English and that helped her a lot. One day I introduced my wife to my single friend. I had told him I was going to my country to get married. He was tempted to get married like me. Three months later, he informed me that he had gone home and had an arranged marriage as well. He invited us to his house and I noticed how happy he and his wife were. I imagined that they must have had very good relations and happy at bedtime! I had a feeling that Sara had talked about her bedtime relations with the wife of my friends and could see a sense of sympathy for her in their eyes. One day my supervisor suggested that he and his wife wanted to come to our house and see my wife. Therefore, I invited him and another lecture to come to my house in two weeks' time. The date was set for a Wednesday evening. I think it was in April. I had asked my married friends to come and help me. His wife was supposed to come to our house and help my wife to cook some dinner. On that morning, we got up at 9 a.m. To my surprise, it was snowing. I wanted to go to the university, fetch my friend, and do some shopping. There were no buses in the street. The snow was so thick that the cars in the street had chains and were driving very slowly. After about an hour or so, a bus came and by the time, I got to the university it was 1 p.m. I asked my friend what to decide? I said wouldn't it be better if I cancelled their visit and asked them to postpone it for some other time? However, he told me not to cancel the meeting. He said his wife would help us to make the party as good as possible. When we returned to my home, it was about 5 p.m. My wife was grumbling and saying why I did not cancel the meeting. Her friend calmed her and said who could forecast such a snow. In the last seven years that I had lived in England, I had not seen such a snow. It was another damn thing happening exactly on the day we wanted to have our guests. Anyway, about 9 p.m. my supervisor and his colleague arrived with their wives. He had brought a bottle of German wine and his friend a bottle of Champagne! Our friend's wife had done all the cooking and had just left. We invited them to our sitting room next to the coal fire we had. The room was quite warm and they talked and talked for quite a while. They appreciated my wife's cooking and the especial dish she had made but they did not know it was made by a professional house wife!

In summer, we received a letter from Sara's brother that he and his mother were coming to visit us. Sara had complained a lot about me to her mother and brother and that was why they wanted to come and see us. Sara's mother had flown to Germany where her son was studying and from there they drove to England with his car, which was a Volkswagen. When they arrived in Sheffield, I was rather glad to see them. Soon I noticed that Sara was welcoming her brother a lot and trying to do all she could for him to make him satisfied. I was becoming jealous of her. After all, I was her husband. He soon left for Germany but my mother-in-law stayed with us for another fortnight.

In August, my supervisor informed that a team of engineers were coming to our university to interview top students to select for a job in an electronic factory. I thought if I get a good job, I might as well stay in England for a few years. In fact, Sara wanted to stay and study for BSc degree if she could. I went for the interview on a Wednesday afternoon. The boss asked me some questions and told his colleagues that this person is the right man for our business. He said he is good in maths and has engineering background. He then told me that you will do apprenticeship for two years and then you should work for us for five years. The plant was somewhere near London. The wage was ninety pounds a month and he said it would increase every year. He asked me if I would agree with their offer. I denied and said I would like to go home after two years. He laughed at me and said we will need you when you become a professional engineer. Now when I think about it I say to myself what an opportunity I had missed. I could have agreed with their offer and after two or three years in case I wanted to return home I could have done so as many my country fellows had done. However, I was honest I think and did not intend to lie or to deceive people.

I had finished my research and my supervisor was very happy with my work. He told me to start writing up my dissertation. The department's secretary was very busy but she introduced a friend of her who was a housewife living near our address. I ringed the typist, made an appointment to go to her house, and explained what I needed. I got to her house as planned at the right time. It was 11 o'clock in the morning of an August day. The weather was quite warm. She invited me to get inside her house. She had two children; one about three years old and the other about a few months old. She was looking after her children while I was explaining about the mathematics formulas. Her baby started crying and she got up and went to feed her. She was dressing a mini skirt and a thin blouse. When she bent to take her child from its cot, I could see her bare thighs and legs. I got excited. When she returned, she noticed my hard breathing. She started breast-feeding her child and by seeing her breasts, I thought she was showing off her body. I wanted to say something to see if she fancied me but then I told myself I was married and she is married too, so there was no point going further. I thought even if she asked for sex relation I would deny it and would tell her that I was a married man and faithful to my wife. Indeed, I had that feeling and since my marriage, I had not visited any street girls. This secretary typed my dissertation on stencil on time. Other times, when visiting her, I never went inside her house. I just waited at the door front and even tried not to look at her eyes directly! Perhaps she did not fancy me at all and all these were a fantasy! I never forget my first meeting of her. It was most pleasurable meeting I ever had.

Later, I wrote a letter to my country Embassy in London and informed them being graduated by the end of September. In my letter, I said I was looking for a job in one of my country's universities; preferably, a university near my hometown. They had passed my latter to the Ministry of Science of my country and soon I received a letter from a university near my hometown; hereafter I call it City University. They needed me and wanted me to work there as an instructor of physics. I was very delighted to have a job fixed for me. My exam was supposed to be on 30th of September. We planned to return by 15th of October. The oral exam with an external examiner took place on time; however, the external examiner had found some mistakes in the proof of a theorem. My supervisor got annoyed and said if it were not because of the good work you had done we would keep you for another term. They gave me a fortnight time to amend my dissertation. I had to change my ticket for first of November.

2-4 Being employed

Sara was upset but to please her I agreed to let her go to Germany to stay with her brother on the 15th of October and I would fetch her on my way to my country from Frankfurt airport. Therefore, she packed up all her belongings in a big suitcase and left other things like books and my clothing to take with me. I took her to London airport on time and when returned I focused on correcting my dissertation. I did it on time and my graduation was approved.

I then set off for home and on the way, Sara got on the plane as was arranged. When she got on the plane, she smiled at me and seemed rather happy. She said she had enjoyed her visit with her brother and had met some friends as well. We did not stay in The Capital and went to The Big City near my hometown straight away. In The Big City near my hometown, we stayed in a hotel. In the afternoon, we slept together; Sara asked me if I had missed her, I said so but when making love once again I was not successful. She got annoyed and told me why I was not hot for her! It had been more than two weeks we had not seen each other. I went to The Big City near my hometown to announce my arrival at City University on the next morning. It was a Wednesday; as the term had started and as my arrival had been postponed, no lectures were set for me. The head of department told me to go and see him on Saturday. We took a bus and went to my hometown. She did not come to my parents' house instead I went to their house. Her mother welcomed me. I slept two nights at their house but we did not make love together. I had a feeling she was dying for bedtime relation and as she found me unwilling was very disappointed. During the past month, I was frustrated and exhausted. I left for The Big City near my hometown on Friday afternoon alone and was given an address of a friend of my brother-in-law to stay with. I stayed with him for a fortnight. It was middle of November and the weather was getting colder and colder. The month of Ramadan had begun and I was fasting as well. I was looking for an apartment or a house to rent. I was told I should attend the university although no classes were set for me. I was told to solve problems for students of a mathematics subject. After two weeks, I went to my hometown for a weekend. I went to Sara's house in the evening. I told her I wanted to fast the next day but in the midnight, she told me I must be crazy because sleeping with her was more important than fasting. Any way we made love together and I did not fast that day. I do not know why I never could satisfy her. By now, I knew she was a very sexy girl and enjoyed bedtime relations a lot but somehow I was not attracted to her. When I was with Lidia, we had sex relation together a lot. She never complained about me being weak or not good at it. However, with Sara she always complained and never said she had enjoyed sex relation with me.

Sara told me the house I rent must have telephone. When I returned to The Big City near my hometown I looked for a house with telephone. In those days, there were few houses in The Big City near my hometown with telephone. Even then, we could not call my hometown from home directly; we had to go to the post office and give our phone number and wait there till they called us. Sara had started making excuses for not coming to The Big City near my hometown and live with me I think. After a month of searching, we found a two-storey house near a posh place of The Big City near my hometown with telephone to rent. It was quite expensive; 200$ per months. My salary was equivalent to 500$. If we had rented an ordinary flat without the phone, the rent would have been much cheaper around 50$. The next thing she wanted was to have a maid. In a weekend in my hometown, we went to find a maid with her sister and mother. Her sister's husband had a car and he drove us to a rural village. We set off about 2 p.m. in the afternoon but he did not find the road, as there were no signs at all. After two hours driving, we were in the middle of nowhere. We found a man on a camel, stopped him and asked the address. He said we had gone the wrong direction. We were lost so we decided to return to my hometown before getting dark and before it gets worse. A few kilometres to my hometown, his car slipped into a mass of sands. We had to get off the car and ask some men to bring a log of wood to get the car out of the sands. It was a terrible experience. In the cold weather of winter evening, frustrated of driving and getting lost and worse of all returning home without finding a maid. This was another sign that things did not turn out as planned. Anyway, my mother promised to find a maid for her. Next time when we went to The Big City near my hometown we took a maid with us. She was middle-aged widower ugly looking and very nosy. Later I noticed that she hid herself behind our bedroom and listened to our talking and whispering. Sometimes I was not successful in making love to Sara and she used to get very annoyed. Shouting and swearing at me and even hitting me why I did not appreciate her beautiful body. There were so many problems in my mind. Our maid was from a poor family. One night I and Sara were invited to a friend's house. When leaving the house I told our maid to be very careful and do not open the door to anybody nor answer the bell. I had a feeling that a thief might come and steel something. In fact, when we returned from the party she said as soon as we had left, someone had jumped over the wall and had stolen some of our clothing; a suite of mine and some of Sara's clothing. She said she had not noticed him coming and when she had heard a noise the thief had run away! I couldn't believe her story. I thought she had a hand with the thief.

Another experience was that Sara told me to write a letter to my father and complain about things that had happened; not paying us more and discriminating between my newlywed sister and me. When I wanted to post the letter my jacket's pocket got stick to a flower pricks and was torn. I thought my letter to my father was too harsh for what he had done for me up to then and that was why my newly sewn jacket was ripped off! In fact he got very annoyed and told his friend not to pay me anymore. There was other things happening which were out of my control and all were rather bad.

The University did not sign an official contract with me until I presented my MSc certificate to them. There was a post office strike in UK, which lasted more than two months. Therefore, I was not paid for a long time. I had to borrow some money from my father's agent. My father had two agents. Both were humorous persons but I was friendlier with the older one. I received my MSc certificate in March. Now in end of February my mother-in-law came to The Big City near my hometown to visit us. I knew Sara had complained a lot about me and told her I was impotent and she did not want to live with me anymore. One day after I had come home from work and was exhausted, my mother-in-law asked me if I loved Sara and wanted to continue my marriage with her. I was surprised to hear that if I didn't want her she would get divorced! I told her I loved my wife and wanted to live with her and would not divorce her at all. She then told her to be obedient and to be kind with me. Sara smiled and told me to go upstairs. It was about 2 o'clock in the afternoon; the upstairs room was cold but the sun was shining inside. We made love in a rush. A month later in March she told me she was pregnant. I was glad to hear that and thought now that she is pregnant she will be busy with her child and would not quarrel with me anymore. Before our New Year, I was paid about 300$. When I cashed the cheque, I was so delighted that I will never forget that moment. Being disappointed, I thought what I could say to my wife now that she is receiving her sister and mother as a guest. Now I had to go to The Capital after the holidays and get my MSc documents certified by the Ministry of Science. As soon as I did that my contract would be signed and my wages would be paid. But I had to wait for five days until our New Year's holidays were over. Sara's family arrived on the eve of our New Year's Day. They were my mother-in-law, sister-in-law, her husband and two of their sons aged three and five. They had their own car. On the New Year's day (it was Thursday as I remember) my mother in law insisted to go to a holly city near The Capital. She wanted to go there and take Sara with her and pray for happiness for her daughter at the moment of our new year. We returned to The Big City near my hometown on the same day. It had taken us four hours to go, some three or four hours to stay there and another four hours to get back. There were seven of us in a car; three in front and four in the rare seat. I think Sara was trapped between her mother, sister and the older sister's son. Back home she was very tired and fell asleep soon. The next three days she was complaining about a pain which was getting worse. On Monday night we took her to a gynaecologist to be examined. He said apparently the foetus is dead and if it is not passed naturally she must have an operation. I had a bus ticket to go to The Capital and pursue my documents to be certified. I forgot to say that I had to do my military service through the university. I was told that after the end of the term I had to start my military service for three months of summer, then teach at the university and do another three months the following year. In the Capital, I had to go to an office opposite to The Capital University and declare that I was ready to do my military service. On Tuesday morning I arrived in The Capital and went to my sister's house. Her husband was a student. Later I went to the Ministry of Science and asked if they had certified my documents. Fortunately, it was ready. I also applied for military notification; I was given a booklet and told that when it is announced by the media I should go and get it stamped; otherwise I should start my service in May instead of 21st of June. I asked the man in charge if I could get it stamped in The Big City near my hometown and he said he didn't see why I couldn't. I returned to The Big City near my hometown on Wednesday with full hand rather happy after five months. But as I got home I was told my wife was in hospital and has had a miscarriage. I rushed to the hospital to visit her but forgot to take any flowers or gifts for her. I told her that I finally had my documents certified and I had the booklet for my military service. She did not admire it and perhaps didn't listen to me at all. Later she had complained that her husband didn't stay with her in the hospital nor he brought any flowers or gifts for her! After the holidays her family went to my hometown and a week later my contract with the university was signed and I was paid quite a big lump of money. Soon I paid the rents for those five months and other debts I had. There was not much money left for me.

We had a neighbour who was a middle aged person with a very beautiful young wife. I guess his wife was twenty years younger than him. Sara got very friendly with them and specially in my absence used to go to their house a lot. They had another family friend; again, the husband was about twenty years older. They invited us a few times and Sara got very friendly with their wives. One night, Sara and our neighbour's wife whose name I cannot remember, were invited to the house of the third party. I and the husbands were in our neighbour's house waiting for them to come home for dinner.

We waited a long time but there were no news from them. Finally, our neighbour sent me there with a chauffeur to take them home. When I got to the address and rang the bell, I could hear them laughing and teasing their husbands. After waiting for more than twenty minutes all of them came out of the house and we took them back home. There was something unusual about them. Later Sara told me as our husbands were all impotent, so they had lesbian acts together. Apparently she had been passive and the other two women active I think. It seemed as if they were drunk as well because were making jokes and laughing most of the time.

Another bad memory in The Big City was that our single friend used to come to our house to visit us more frequently. Later on I noticed that each time he comes to see us he tries to be very posh and well dressed. He also tried to get my wife pleased by telling jokes and being humorous as well. One day we were walking along the river bank and I saw Sara just wanting to talk to him and to be with him. At home I got very annoyed with her; in response she said when you cannot satisfy me sexually what do you expect. I want to have sex relation with a young strong man and enjoy myself. She said she did not enjoy being with me anymore. I do not know if she was unfaithful to me or not, but after getting friendlier with those two women I think she did not try to be with other men as she used to be. In one occasion, we had come to my hometown for a weekend and were invited by her aunt. At her aunt's house, a cousin of her was there as well. Sara had told me that she wanted to get married with him but apparently, his father had said he was too young to get married. I guess by her impressions that she had had some kind of intimate relation with her cousin. Anyway Sara and her cousin were talking together in front of me and their mothers and telling jokes and teasing each other so much that I was blushed and really annoyed. I didn't know what to say and what to do. I was quiet all the time; I am a quiet person anyway.

Spring of 1971 was full of bad memories. Sometimes I tried a lot to be very friendly with Sara, but I don't know why anything that happened made our relations worse. In March, my eldest uncle had a very bad car accident and was taken to a hospital in the Capital. On the 20th of April, radio announced that all the academics who had obtained a booklet for military service should go to The Capital and get their booklet stamped for June. Otherwise, they would be regarded as absent. On the 21st of April I went to the military office in The Big City near my hometown and asked them to stamp my booklet as the sergeant in The Capital had told me a month before. They said the booklet is stamped only in The Capital and all the candidates from all over the country should go there. I took a bus in the evening and went to the Capital. In the morning, I went to the military office opposite to The Capital University. I was not allowed to get inside, instead I was told to write my request and hand it to the guard. To get the reply I had to come again in a week's time. I asked my sister's husband to go and get the response for me. Later I was informed that I had been present and there is no need to worry. My sister's husband had told them that I was absent and my booklet was not stamped but they insisted that they had reported me as present!

In June, her behaviour was getting worse and we quarrelled every day. She used to make me very annoyed and sometimes we hit each other fiercely. Later our maid had reported this to my mother and said that in one occasion Sara nearly had killed me! One weekend on our visit to my hometown, she had received a letter from her brother in Germany. He had invited her to go to Germany and stay with him and continue her studies. She told me that she wanted to get divorced and did not want to come to The Big City any more. Although her mother persuaded her to come with me to The Big City, but I noticed that she was grumbling more and more and getting intolerable more and more as every day passed. On the 14th of June, her mother came to The Big City and said she is taking her daughter to our hometown because I was due to start my military service in the Capital. First thing we rang the landlord and told him we are going to evacuate the house. He charged us a month extra rate because our contract was for one year. This was an extra pressure on me. Later her mother decided to collect all Sara's belongings and send it to our hometown. On the 17th of June they went to our hometown and I went to The Capital to start my military service. She never came back to live with me. She had decided to get divorced and I was so frustrated and emotionally down that I wished this could happen as soon as possible.

On the 18th of June I went to the military office once more in The Capital, however, I was not let in. I was told to go to another office. I was very desperate, knew no one and had no one to help me. I went to the other military office and wanted to show my booklet to someone and explain what had happened. In that desperate mood, suddenly someone called me by first name and came out of his office. I didn't recognize him but he said we were schoolmates in the first year of elementary school. He said he had seen me in my hometown when I was young but I couldn't remember him at all. Anyway he said he was doing his military service as an officer in that office and asked me what he could do for me. I was very delighted to hear that. After all those soreness and unhappy events, it was the first good thing I had come across. I explained my situation and he wrote a note, sent me back to the other office with a soldier, and told him to do their best for me. In return to the other office I was allowed to get inside and explain my status. The officer in charged told me I was supposed to be present but I explained that I had not come to their office on the date announced by radio and gave him the booklet to check. He then checked all the names; to our surprise, there was another person with the same surname as me but different first name. His name was recorded five names before my name, so each time the officer had checked the names he had come across with his name and had not continued to check other names. It was a rare occasion; in between more than 140 names only two candidates had the same surnames. The officer took me to a General and explained what had happened. He then ordered my booklet to be stamped. When coming out of the office I was very delighted and relieved. Someone like an angel had appeared out of nowhere to rescue me from being absent and overdoing the military service and further misery. The next day which was a Wednesday, I went to the military camp and declared myself as present. They cut our hair as short as possible and gave us boots and garments and sent us home to give the garment to the tailor to make necessary tailoring. They told us to go to the main campus in the East of The Capital on Friday evening, to be divided in groups, and to show what we had to do from Saturday. The start of the military service was very hard for all of us. My companions were all academic staff from different universities across my country; I was the youngest only twenty-five years old. Most of them had their PhD's and were middle aged. Among them were a few very famous persons. There were two other persons from my University, a physician and a chemist. On Friday evening we were lined in rows of eight and divided into two brigades. We were told to go to bed at half past eight in the evening and to get up at four o'clock in the morning. The officer in charge of us was very serious and restrictive to us. Other officers working under him seemed very serious in the first place but later became rather friendly. We had to sleep rather very early, some colleagues couldn't sleep and tried to keep talking, making jokes and make us laugh, however, the surgeons checking us shouted to be quiet and to sleep. At about nine o'clock everybody was quiet and we soon fell asleep. At four o'clock in the morning we were woken up by the whistle of the officer. He shouted we should get up and be dressed in one minute. It only took more than one minute to wear boots and fasten the straps alright! He whistled again and told us to rush. He gave us half an hour to go to the toilets and get washed. There were six toilets and about seventy of us in one camp. Then we were lined again and lead to the dining room where breakfast was served. About six o'clock we were lined and marched to the main square to marsh in front of the head of the campus. There were apparently ten thousand soldiers in this camp and it took about two hours to see the parade. Another two hours were spent learning military rules. At ten o'clock we had a break for an hour. In break time we went to a free shop to buy milk or a piece of cake. There was a big queue, but drinking cold milk in hot summer weather was very refreshing. Soon I met a friend who was a physician. He was a very kind and friendly person. The first week was very awful. I was very depressed and worried about my future. The married soldiers could go home on Monday evenings if they wished but we were allowed to leave the camp on Wednesday evenings and had to return to the camp on Friday evening before six o'clock. I think I didn't leave the camp on first few Monday evenings, but later I left the camp in one or two occasions. During weekends I used to go either to my grandfather's house or my sisters' house.

3-4 Getting divorced

After four weeks doing military service, I went to my hometown on a Wednesday evening and got there on Thursday morning. After visiting my parents, I went to Sara's house. She welcomed me. She took me to their underground which was rather colder than other rooms. She brought some breakfast for me and then she said she wanted her divorce, she said she had decided to go to abroad and study there. I told her I had missed her and wanted to make love to her one more time. She said she would rather ask her mother first. She came back after a few minutes, said she was a good wife, and so would obey me. As I did not have any preservative with me she said she is obedient but to prevent pregnancy suggested a different method. It seemed odd to me but the experience was very memorable indeed. I had tried not to abuse myself during last month and I think our affair lasted about a minute. It was enjoyable for both of us. About ten o'clock we came out of the room, I told her I wanted to go home. Her mother turned out and told me Sara wants her divorce. I said I would divorce her if she wants so; her mother asked if I would pay her dowry (the marriage money agreed at the time of marriage) and I said I would honour that. Then I went home. My father was doing his prayers when I arrived. I told him my wife wants to get divorced and I had agreed. He seemed very worried but he said if it makes you happy he would be happy with that as well. My eyes were full of tears; I told him I had had a very hard life during the past eighteen months and that I thought Sara did not want to live with me anymore. I was worried about dowry and he said not to worry about it. I had told my wife that I would return in two weeks' time and do what was required for getting divorced formally. On my return to my hometown, her sister's husband came in and said we had to go to the court and agree with the divorce. I accompanied them to the court. The judge asked me why I wanted to divorce her and I said we haven't been able to live together in peace and although she is a good girl I cannot tolerate living with her anymore. The judge told me I could refuse divorcing her because he doesn't see any good reason for the divorce. I said I was quite happy with divorcing her and she also gave her consent for the divorce. The judge told me to think about it and said he gives me one-month time to reconsider my decision. We left the court, both seemed happy for our decision. This was the last time I saw Sara. I went back to the Capital. I gave my father the right to sign the divorce documents on my behalf in my absence. Our divorce took place officially in beginning of August 1971. It happened almost two years after breaking with Lidia. What a harsh and difficult time I had in the last two years. I think all these events were because I had broken Lidia's heart. I always thought I was so happy with Lidia. She never blamed me for bedtime relations or being a weak person regarding lovemaking. In fact it had never occurred to me that I was to some degree impotent. I had confidence in myself and before getting married with Sara I even thought I was very potent indeed (a hot pot as a London prostitute had called me!). However, with Sara I was called all sorts of things; weak, idiot, impotent, not eager for women and so on. With Lidia, I always had my smile on my face but with Sara, I always looked worried and exhausted. Now, I wish I had stayed with Lidia for all my life and wish I had never thought about other women! I know I had abused myself from childhood, but I could not figure out why Lidia was content with me while Sara was not. That summer was a hard life for me. The military service was also tough and harsh for me. Although, I found some good friends there, I did not tell them about divorcing my wife and pretended to have a good married life. I came across with a physician who was very friendly with me. I also came to know an ear, nose and throat specialist. I arranged to have a nose operation on a Thursday morning without letting my parents or other members of my family know.

4-4 Back in The Big City near my hometown

I returned to The Big City near my hometown on the 20th of September. I found a new apartment to rent. It was the second floor of a house rather far from the university, but the rent was cheap. The rent was only about 40.00$ per month. Besides, my mother sent a maid for me to do the house work. She was a divorcee; an ugly woman in her forties with an eight-year-old daughter. She was a very kind woman anyway. She did all the house work for me. This included shopping, washing, ironing, cleaning, cooking and serving meals on time. With her I didn't have to bother about these problems. First thing I did I sent her daughter to school. Of course, I paid her money as well, every month. Now I could save some money. I had decided to be a good boy, not to abuse myself any more, but it did not last very much. After about three months, a student of mine told me there is a pimp lady who introduces beautiful and young street girls. First time that I rang her was a Wednesday afternoon. I told her who had introduced me and that I did not have a car. She asked me to go to an address she gave and fetch a girl from there. Those days mobile phones were not available yet and I did not have phone in my new apartment, so I used public phones. Anyway, I met this girl just on time I was supposed to do. To my surprise she carried her daughter who was about five years old with her. Apparently she had got divorced and had to do this for her living.

She was a very beautiful girl. We went to my apartment by a taxi. My maid had left the house with her daughter and I knew she wouldn't come for more than two hours. The house owners were inside their apartment and the house was very quiet. We went up the stairs very quietly. I turned the television on and her daughter stayed in the hall watching television. We went to my bedroom. I didn't have a bed that time. Just I spread what was called a bed on the floor and had a good time with her; she did not show any enthusiasm although she was young; our lovemaking lasted a few minutes as usual. She was really beautiful with an innocent look and her figure was like one of cinema's artists. I cannot remember how much I paid her. I accompanied her down the stairs and told her I wanted to see her again, however, I never saw her again. When my maid returned she had a feeling that I had taken a girl into the apartment. Later she said a young man should get married, I agreed with her and said I was divorced already but if I find a good woman, I would marry her. That agent friend of my father soon found a divorcee for me. He said she belongs to a rich family, she has a two year old son and her parents would support me financially if I marry with their daughter. I told the story to my mother and asked her to come and see the woman. We went to their house as arranged with my mother and my maid to see this girl. She was about the same age as I was, but was rather plump. She was not very beautiful but I think she was on the average side. I thought she would fit me; especially that we were in the same boat; I mean both of us had unsuccessful marriage. I didn't ask her why she was divorced nor did she ask me. My mother did not like her at all and was very impatient to leave their house. Back at home she disagreed with me marrying her and her main reason was her child. Her parents had told us they would look after her child but my mother said after a few months they would send her child to her mother and would not keep their promise. She was rather upset with this proposal and said not to hurry, she would find me a suitable girl. In another occasion a religious friend offered me a girl from a rather poor family. When she introduced her later, I noticed that she was one of my students. She was rather slim and coloured. I didn't like his offer and did not pursue the case any further. This academic year passed quickly as well. I had some problems regarding my teaching with students, but I had to give concessions to the students and take the exams easy and give them good marks. I had become very friendly specially with the students in the evening classes who were mostly school teachers continuing their studies towards a higher degree to be able to teach in high schools.

I had one or two more experience with street girls in this apartment. One day my maid said that the landlord has a daughter who is a teacher and is a university graduate and they would like to get to know me better. In one occasion they invited me to go to a garden with their family. My maid was invited too. We accepted their invitation and stayed with them for a full day. There were all of her family there; her brothers and sisters. Apparently, she had lost her father. They tried to play volleyball there and invited me to play with them as well. I didn't like the atmosphere at all and wanted to get back home as soon as possible. In the evening, my maid asked me if I fancied the girl for marriage and I said I didn't like her at all; I said she had thick legs! The next day she had examined her figure carefully and told me I was right. She said I had a deep insight into girls' figures. As time passed by I was getting fitter and more and more feeling better. I was not as depressed as the previous year when I was with Sara. In June I packed my baggage and left it in my father's agent house. I gave the apartment back and went to The Capital to do the rest of my military service during the summer. My maid stayed with a hometown family.

On June the 20th I started my second term military service and spent the summer in the same brigade for three months. This time the physicians were not with us and we were only the scientists; about eighty personnel. I have mixed memories. During my military service in summer 1972, I came across with a mate who took me to one of his relatives. He was about forty years old and a single person from a rich family. He didn't have a job; only he had a lot of apartments and some agricultural lands in nearby villages. His income was from the rents of these apartments and he was relatively well off. His house was newly built in a posh area with many rich people around it. He had an ordinary car. He was a pleasant person and first time I met him was with his cousin. Actually, I became very friendly with him and most Thursdays I arranged to go and see him in his house. He had a lot of call girls and often used to call one of them to come to his house. Usually, it took about an hour or so before they arrived after he ringed them. One of these girls was a tall slim and very beautiful girl. Her figure was like film actors and used to make jokes; a very lovely girl. She charged each of us equivalent to 20 dollars. Each time she came, my friend cooked something for dinner and we really enjoyed our time with her. I have been with a few very beautiful women but it has cost me a lot of money, time and energy. Besides, the enjoyment lasted for a short time say ten to twenty minutes. It was a kind of self- abusing also a kind of addiction for me. Anyway, my contact with my friend lasted after my military service and in summers of 1973 and 1974 when in the Capital, I used to ring him and arrange to go to his house and have a good time with the prostitutes he used to invite. I remember this pretty girl saying that although I was not good at sex but she liked to see me so excited and this gave her a hidden pleasure. Maybe she said this to make me happy. I remember the days when I used to go to London to see Valerie she also told me I was not good at sex but she said she enjoyed being with me because I was a hot pot!

After finishing the military service, I returned to The Big City near my hometown and tried to find an apartment to live in. My father's agent helped me to find a house and by going to an agency, I managed to rent an apartment in a very posh area of The Big City near my hometown. It was a two-storey house; the owners were living in the ground floor and the top floor was let for rent to me. It consisted of a small hall, two bedrooms, a large room for guests, a bathroom, a toilet and a big kitchen. It had a nice view both in front and in the rare. My maid occupied the bedroom next to the kitchen and I selected the front bedroom. Soon my belongings were brought to this house and we got it furnished alright. They were a quiet family and I seldom met them. Only when paying the rent I usually gave a cheque to my maid to pay the landlord. In September 1973 I met the landlord after one year. He asked me to increase the rent and I agreed. As soon as I settled down in this apartment, I sent my maid's daughter to school. She was in the second year of the school now and her mother was very happy for her daughter going to school. After a few months, I ringed the pimp whom I had kept her phone number. She sent me a slut. She was a tall girl with a beautiful figure. She was also nice looking but her breasts were not so firm. We became very friendly soon. When I first met her, she was about the same age as me; 25 or 26 years old. She used to come to The Big City near my hometown once a month and later I gave her a key in case she arrived late in the night. My maid also liked her and each time she came to visit me she usually stayed for lunch or supper and sometimes stayed one or two nights with me. She always gave me a quick sex and slept with me till morning. My life in this apartment was passing by peacefully and with pleasure. Even then, if I felt I needed sex I used to call the pimp. Nearly once or sometimes twice a week I had sex relation with the call girls.

I had an evening student who wore thick glasses and seemed to be well off. Later I noticed that he run a newspaper shop in a crowded Street. He also sold books and magazines and I noticed that he also sold the Play Boy magazine. I asked for this magazine and he told me he had porno magazines with hard porno photographs. He told me not to be shy and he was keen on porno magazines himself. I bought a magazine and every time he brought new issues I was his customer. They cost a lot but the magazines were beautiful and each time I looked over the porn photographs, it ended with self- abusing. Once I brought in my house a middle-aged woman and to get her excited I showed her this magazine. She got really excited and gave me a good job. She was a simple woman; I remember she said it is a shame that these women have allowed a photographer to take these pornographic photos!

In the summer of 1973, I went to my hometown and as I remember I stayed in the village with my parents for a month I think. On my return I applied for a grant to go abroad to study for a PhD degree. I contacted my MSc supervisor asking him to advise me what to do. He recommended me to a University Professor he knew, so I applied for a place. They soon sent me a letter of acceptance to read for engineering. I met our Dean and told him I wanted to read for engineering degree. He refused first, but finally accepted my request as I insisted a lot and agreed with it. Only I had to wait until my military service card was issued. I was told I could go to UK to continue my studies from September 1974.

From September 1973 to August 1974 my life in The Big City near my hometown was more or less the same as the year before that. From January 1974 my enthusiasm for call girls had increased. I invited them at least twice a week. In some occasions, some of them showed their desire to get married with me. As soon as I noticed this, I did not go out with them anymore. The most friendly one used to come to my house a lot and had become so friendly that she thought she was the lady of the house. Other friends and colleagues wanted to find someone for me to get married. Especially now that I was going to study abroad, more people were thinking of introducing someone they knew. Two occasions I never forget. First case, we had a colleague whose wife was very beautiful. One day he said my wife has a cousin who is educated and we think she suits you very much. So they arranged a meeting at their house. I had the vision of his wife in my mind, but when I saw this poor girl, I could not imagine marrying her. Her eyes were squint and ignoring that she was not as beautiful as her cousin was. Later I told my colleague that I did not intend to get married now. Second case was a beautiful student from a rich family. Two of my colleagues had gone for proposal and her parents had rejected them. A colleague of mine who had some relation with this girl took me to his room and said if you fancy this girl just let me know. I told him why you offer her for me. He said you are from a rich family; you are educated and gentle, I rely on you and am sure you will be a happy couple. I refused and said two of my colleagues have made proposals for this girl and I know one of them insists and it is not right for me to go ahead. This was an excuse; my fear was my weakness in bedtime.

5-4 Going abroad again

In June of 1974, I went to my hometown. I told my mother that I wanted get married and take my wife with me to UK. My mother tried few places but was unsuccessful. I told my mother that now that I am going to UK I would see if I could find someone like Lidia; if so I would marry an English girl. She groaned a bit but did not give any comments. In fact I had decided to look for a British girl for marriage. I had concluded that no one would be better for me than my old girlfriend would, but I was ashamed to make a proposal to her even if I could find her. I wanted to look for someone like her!

I had applied for a place to live in halls of residence of Southern University. My supervisor had contacted the accommodation office and had asked them to reserve a room for me from the beginning of the term.

On my arrival in Southern which is a suburb of Liverpool, I got a taxi and went to the address I was given. It was called The Village. It consisted of sixty houses. Each house had eleven bedrooms; three rooms on the first floor and four rooms on the second and third floor. The extra place on the first floor was occupied by a bathroom, which had three showers and a tube. A kitchenette was on the second floor. The Village accommodated both girls and boys. The front houses were let to the girls and the rare ones to the boys. A river passed through the Village. The Warden's office was in the front and there were plenty of parking spaces for those who owned a car. I soon settled down in my room which was on the first floor (ground floor) of the house. Opposite to me was an Egyptian student doing PhD in Chemical Engineering. On my left side was a student from Nigeria and in the other room was a British student. I lived in The Village for one and a half year.

6-4 Life in the village from September1974- March 1976

After settling in the Village, I decided not to look for street girls and not to abuse myself either. I did not go out searching for street girls for a month or two. Abusing myself had become a bad habit for me and although I used a lot of effort to leave this habit, but my decisions did not work out after a few days. There were quite a few compatriots in the Village; most of them were doing either MSc or PhD although there were a few reading for BSc degree. I came to know a student, doing PhD in chemistry, an undergraduate student reading for BSc in Mechanical Engineering and another one, a PhD student doing chemistry. Two of them who I was more friendly with them took me one night to a casino club very close to the Village. I had a small bet that night and I won. However, I had decided not to gamble anymore and not to bet on horses either. However, this decision did not last much and soon I bought newspapers and spent a lot of my time studying the horses' records and going to betting offices, which many of them were around us. Usually I used to walk to the university in the mornings and it took about half an hour. I used to walk back home in the evenings and seldom took a bus. I made a pass to some English girls in one or two occasions but my attempts were unsuccessful. Besides, I was studying on my own in an office room at the university and did not attend any courses, so I hardly met any girls in working hours. I concluded that I couldn't find an English girl suitable for marriage; the girls I had met were very experienced and my illusion of my old girlfriend was now just a dream. I decided to get married with a compatriot girl next summer I go home.

One Saturday evening in November, the weather was quite cold and I had decided not to go out. I was studying deep and had concentrated on reading a scientific paper. At about eight o'clock I heard a knock on the door. I opened the door. A girl asked me if I knew when my Nigerian neighbour would come home. I told her I had no clue. She said she was supposed to see him at eight o'clock and said if I didn't mind she would wait for him in my room till he comes. I let her inside. She said she was hungry and I brought some bread, butter and cheese for her. Also gave her a cup of tea. She talked in slang. She had blue eyes and a little make up over her face. Her eyebrows were quite thick. She was in her twenties but looked like a teenager; perhaps because of her eyebrows. She looked a very simple girl. After a while, she asked me if I did business. I understood what she meant and said why not. She asked for only two pounds and we had a quick action. I gave her two pounds and before she left, she asked me if she could come and see me more. I had decided not to look for street girls or prostitutes. I wondered my fate was written with these poor women! I thought I needed to relieve myself occasionally and now that a girl had come to my room with her own feet why not accept her. Her name was Vickie and soon she became a steady friend with me. I used to go out a lot with her and in the Village I was often seen accompanying her. Her home was not too far from the Village. She was a bit soft minded and had gone out with many students in the Village. Later when she became friendlier with me, she also brought some of her friends who were short of money and needed money badly. My relation with Vickie lasted for quite a while, in fact until I left the Village and went to my country for getting married in March 1976. Vickie was a good sex partner and whenever I needed her, she was there. She never stayed a whole night with me. She was afraid of her parents and used to say her mother did not allow her to stay away at night time. Meanwhile, I had bought a bicycle for forty pounds and I used to go to the university by riding the bicycle. One Friday afternoon I rode to a suburb. I had seen some strange adverts in local newspapers and had guessed that it was related to models as they said. Any way I soon found the address and saw a woman in her thirties standing at her door front. Her looks was the looks of a prostitute! I parked my bicycle at a corner and came to her and asked her if she did business. Her response was positive. I went to her flat had a quick sex relation and paid her two pounds as I remember. I drove back home somehow pleased and relieved. Besides having Vickie, I used to go to other areas occasionally looking for street girls. Some of them were quite nice while some were not nice at all. I was satisfied with the service they gave me.

In March I bought a B&O stereo phonic radio cassette player for 270 pounds. It was a very expensive set and as my supervisor had told me it was the best and the most expensive one in the market. I also bought a second hand car. It was a Mini. For driving it I went to a driving school and told them I had a British Driving License but had not driven a car since I had got the Licence in 1969. Soon I got familiar with driving. In 1976 I looked for street girls more often. I have many memorable stories with street girls while in Southern. I had found the address and phone number of one of these so called models. I used to buy Swedish Porno magazines, which were very beautiful indeed. They were published in Sweden and were sent to me by mail. The paper, photography and the stories were excellent indeed.

In summer 1975, I had decided to go home and get married. I had written a letter to my mother and asked her to find someone for me to get married with when I go home in summer. Just a week before leaving Liverpool, I had given my car to a mechanic to do some repairs. It was a Friday afternoon about 3 p.m. that I went to the mechanic and got my car. I paid for the repairs and wanted to drive the car and see how it was. Near the Village, a car overtook me and I was challenged to follow him. I accelerated and was exceeding the speed limit. When trying to overtake a bus in the bus stop, suddenly I noticed an old man was running towards the bus. There was a workshop across the street and the workers had just finished their work and were getting on the bus. The poor man hit the car. As soon as I saw him I made an emergency break, but it was too late. He had hit the front boot and the front window of the car. The window broke and he fell on the street. I pulled off and stopped my car in front of the bus. Soon an ambulance arrived and two police cars also came to check the scene of the accident. I was taken to a police car and questioned. I told them I was exceeding the speed limit and I thought I was driving at 40 miles an hour. Another policeman was examining the break line and came to me saying that my tyres were rather old. I told him I had just got my car from the mechanics and showed him the receipt of the mechanic. This policeman was rather kind and told me not to worry. He said although I was driving fast and rather carelessly, but he reckoned the man had not crossed the zebra crossing and so he thought it was his fault for the accident. I think he was right, because the car in front of me had just overtook the bus also exceeding the speed limit safely. I signed the documents the police presented and then they told me I was free to go home. I told the police officer I had planned to go to my country in a week's time and he said it's alright as long as I attend the court on my return which would be in October. Anyway, that night I could not sleep well because I was thinking if I were approved to be guilty for the accident, perhaps I would be prisoned. I went to London to arrange for my trip. In London, I visited my friend from The Big City near my hometown who had come from USA and was going to my country for summer holidays. I took him to a posh restaurant in Kensington Street. He was very kind and a real gentle man. I still have contacts with him and in some occasions he has been very helpful to me. I consider him as a very sincere friend of mine. My friend told me not to worry about the accident and tried to make jokes and make me happy. A week later, I flew home and soon I went to my hometown to visit my parents. In the summer, we went to the nearby village as usual. I told my mother that I had decided to get married this summer and take someone with me to UK on my return as a wife but since I had made an accident and was waiting for the court hearing in October, I had changed my mind and did not want to get married then. I told her to keep on looking for me and let me know of her decision.

When I returned to Southern, a lawyer from the insurance company came to see me and told me I could attend the court or leave it up to him. I was found guilty for careless driving and fined five pounds. I was relieved a lot. I bought a brand new Mini car for thirteen hundred pounds. I liked this car very much, its colour was bracken and I believed it brought good luck for me. With this car I travelled a lot, went to London and Birmingham quite a lot. Also went to Manchester to meet prostitutes. However, I was still looking for street girls and sometimes I visited the massage rooms. I had bought a Polaroid camera, which printed photos on a special paper fed into it in just a minute or two. The quality of the pictures was poor but it was handy and I liked it very much. In one occasion I arranged to meet a prostitute in her flat. I took this camera with me. I told her it was my desire to get photos of her while we were love making. She didn't object and I took some photos of her while she was naked and trying to make love to me. The photos didn't turn out to be clear and when I was going to get married I tore them off. She was a very kind woman but I did not see her any more. Probably she had changed her address.

CHAPTER 5

I-5 Getting married again

Just before Christmas holidays I received a letter from my mother in which they had sent me the photograph of a girl. My mother said in her letter that she knew the family of this girl; especially her cousin. I took the photo from the envelope and examined it carefully. It was a nice black and white photo and I responded to my mother's letter immediately. In my letter, I said that I liked the photo and I thought this was my ideal girl for marriage. I said I could come home in March and get married during our new year's holidays. My parents responded soon and said they had arranged for the wedding as I had suggested. One day I went to see my friend who was seven years older than I was and was still single. I told him I was going to get married in March and said that it was an arranged marriage. He asked me if I knew the girl, or knew her parents. I told him I hadn't seen the girl and did not know her parents either. He told me I was very stupid! I said why and he said because you have had an unsuccessful marriage before and still believe in old ideas. I didn't like his comments and told him I cannot wait any longer to be single. I told him I want to get married and form a family. Later he told me he had written a letter to his parents blaming them not letting him to marry the girl he wanted. Apparently his parents had responded that they would not object with him marrying and would be glad to help him financially or otherwise for his marriage. He was tempted to get married soon!

From the time I confirmed the proposal to the time I had planned go home and get married was about three months left. I decided not to abuse myself and not to pursue street girls; but I could not help myself. I registered in a bodybuilding club. I attended this club three times a week between two to three o'clock in the afternoons. Two months was a short period to make a major effect on me. I was getting greedier for sex relation somehow and I thought I must get most of my time enjoying with street girls. I had a car now and sometimes picked a girl in a club or along streets. As time passed by and I was getting closer to the time of going home and getting married I was getting greedier and just a week before going to my country I had several experience with street girls.

Just a month before my departure, my fiancé's uncle came to London with a friend and I drove to London to see him. I met him in a hotel and there I gave him a letter to pass to my wife to be. In that letter which was written on a nice paper with a green color envelope I said I couldn't wait to get married with her. She replied to my letter. A very short letter in which there was no sign of enthusiasm for seeing me. In two or three more letters that I wrote, I explained how much I missed her. I also sent her a couple of photographs but received none. Just a week before my departure, I went to Birmingham to see my friend and to consult with his wife for doing some shopping. I also went to a hairdresser but I did not want to dye my grey hair. My friend's wife insisted to dye my hair; I told her I wanted my fiancé to see me as I was but she said you must look like a groom. I had bought a velvet navy colored suit with a bow tie for myself. Just ten days before our new year, I arrived in the Capital. I went to my grandfather's house before going to my hometown. I told my grandfather that shopping and spending money is very enjoyable, but he said earning money and saving it is much more enjoyable than spending it.

2-5 Getting married again! (March 1976)

On 11th of March I arrived in my hometown. I remember it was Thursday. My mother told me to ring the bride's house and inform them I had arrived. I think my fiancé took the phone and as soon as I introduced myself, she gave the phone to her mother. She seemed to be nervous on the phone and said would see me on Saturday. On Saturday evening, my mother, sisters and I went to their house to see the bride. On their side were her mother, aunt and her uncle's wife. The women were all wearing hijabs and I was wearing a new suit, with a tie. I think I looked quite handsome in new clothes. We talked a bit with her family for a while when the bride to be arrived in a red dress. She came towards me and we shook hands together. She sat next to me looked a bit nervous and rather blushed but soon smiled and we started talking about television programs and the magazines. I asked her what type of songs she liked, and who were her favorite singers. We talked for more than half an hour while my mother was talking about the wedding ceremony with her mother. Back at home, my father asked me what I thought about the bride. I told him she was too young, she had not finished the high school and that I wanted a woman only five or six years younger than me. He said how stupid I was. He said all men want to marry with very young girls. In our culture, fourteen-year-old girls are the most wanted and is the best age for lovemaking. I didn't say anything else but I thought she was too young for me. Two days later I went to a clinic for blood test with my brother. I saw a tall man with a young girl wearing hijab and a young boy standing next to a tree apparently waiting for their turn for blood test. My brother told me these are your relatives; the bride, her father and brother. I hadn't seen her father and brother before. I was shocked, I think they were shocked as well because neither of us was wearing good clothes and neither of us expected to see the other side in the clinic. Later my wife said her father had asked her if I was one of her teachers. Perhaps he didn't expect me to be thirty years old.

On Thursday afternoon (19th of March 1976), I, my father, brothers with my brother-in-laws went to their house. On the way, we picked a neighbor and someone drove us to their house. We got there about half past three in the afternoon. We were guided to a small room. On their side were her father, and uncles; also some other men whom I didn't know. After an hour or so two religious leaders of my hometown who were very prestigious arrived. One of them would present me and the other one the bride for reading the marriage ceremony. The bride wasn't ready. She was taken to a hairdresser for make-up. She arrived too late and I remember the Mullah who was supposed to represent me was getting nervous and saying if it gets dark the wedding would be deemed. I didn't appreciate his comments although I knew he wanted to urge them to prepare the ceremony as soon as possible. At about eight o'clock we were told the bride had arrived and the Mullahs could perform the ceremony. The older Mullah went to the ladies room to get concession of the bride and returned after half an hour. Then the other Mullah asked my permission to read the verses in Arabic with the bride's representative and the registrar brought his book of registration and wrote down the agreements. The registrar asked me what I would designate for the bride's wedding and as we had agreed, I told him half of the land I had in The Big City near my hometown. Then they brought the registration document to be signed by me and four witnesses, two on my side and two on the bride's side. The Mullahs left the house and the ceremony started. I was taken to the bride's room and a photographer took some photos while the house was full of ladies and children who had come to see the bride and the groom closely. Later they gave us especial dinner. At about 11 o'clock we were taken to our house by my uncle's car. My wife and I sat in the front seat of the car and in the rear seat; there were her mother, aunts and someone else whom I did not know. At the gate of our house, our servant had a sheep ready to be killed and as soon as we got off the car, he killed the poor sheep. It was a custom as well to sacrifice a sheep to keep the devil eyes off the ceremony. The photographer was ready and took plenty of photographs of the ceremony. As soon as we got inside the guest room, my brothers who were seventeen years old, had a record player ready and turned it on with some music played especially for wedding ceremonies. They started dancing and my sisters joined them dancing. Also they asked me and my wife to dance. This dancing lasted for half an hour or so and then my mother-in-law said they must be tired. The ceremony finished and I and my wife were led to the bedroom which was nicely decorated for us. Before going to bed, my wife changed her wedding dress in another room and entered the bed with a night dress which I had brought from UK. They closed the bedroom door and we were left alone. I noticed that my mother-in-law with my wife's aunts (two of them) were going to sleep in the next room. It was also a custom for the bride's close relatives to sleep nearby the groom's bedroom just in case the bride was hurt during deflowering, they could help and bring in first aid if necessary. It was about one o'clock in the morning when we went to bed. I held my hand under her neck and kissed her for a while. She said she was very tired and it had been a very busy day for her. I said I was tired too and soon we fell asleep. In the morning we got off about eight o'clock. We were served breakfast. My wife relatives said something to my wife, presumably asked her about our bed time. Later my mother told me that she had told them her son was educated abroad and knew that he shouldn't disturb the bride when she is too tired. On Friday we went outside together to visit my relatives who had come from far away. My grandfather, my uncles and my aunts were among the guests. On Friday night we went to bed at about ten o'clock. We were left alone and no one slept in the nearby room. Everything was prepared for me to get on with the especial ceremony; that is deflowering the bride. I tried to get her undressed which she did not mind. I was excited for a short time but as getting her ready took some time I noticed I was losing my excitement quickly. I was telling her the story of my journey that I noticed she had fallen asleep. I didn't wake her up and slept next to her till morning. Early in the morning, I got my excitement back but she was fast asleep and I thought not to bother her, so she was not deflowered on the second night either. On Saturday, it was 21st of March; our new year's day. We went to their house to give our greetings to her parents. On Saturday night I couldn't deflower her again. Some wrong thinking was attacking my mind. I was getting rather depressed. She lied down next to me like a log without showing any emotions! I did not get excited at all. She didn't refuse or deny me either. It looked as if she was told to surrender and let it happen, no matter what. Only in the mornings, I was excited but she was fast asleep then and I did not dare to wake her up. Two more nights passed the same. On Tuesday morning my mother asked me why I had not done my job (deflowering) and I said I didn't know why it didn't happen. She gave me a tablet and said the servant had obtained it from the chemist shop. I took the tablets in the evening; my wife noticed it but didn't say anything. Later she always blamed my mother and the servant for what they had done. She still believes that if I was not given those tablets she would have remained virgin and could have asked for divorce immediately. She is right; however, the tablets didn't help. Mind you the Viagra tablets were not produced yet. In early hours of our sleep, I told her some jokes and stories but then again I did not get excited at all. In early morning about five o'clock I was excited. I tried to waken her up but she turned round and fell fast asleep. I had decided to deflower her. Therefore, I got close to her from behind and deflowered her. She did not say anything. She wasn't hurt either and there was no sign of bleeding as what I had seen from Sara. I was not sure that I had done the job completely. We had arranged to go to the photographer and take some passport size photos. The photographer took some extra pictures of us. Whenever I look at those photos I can see the anxiety in my eyes. I never forget that day. However, on our return to our home, my mother took me aside and congratulated me for what I had done. I asked her what's she congratulating me for and with a look of surprise she said my son you have finally deflowered your bride successfully. I couldn't believe it and asked her how come; she said they could see the signs on the bed. As soon as my mother told me I was a man I obtained my pride back and all my anxieties about bed time relations diminished quickly. In the afternoon when we went to our bedroom to have a nap we made love together. She neither refused me nor did she show any sign of enjoyment or excitement. She just lied down (like a log!) and let me to make love to her. Later she admitted she thought she had to surrender and let the husband get on with it. She said she never enjoyed having sex relation with me because she was never aroused by me nor I did my lovemaking properly. She blamed me that as soon as she wanted to show sign of enjoyment I had finished.

Of course, she was right. As I had been with prostitutes and as they like their side to finish the job as quickly as possible and get their money, I was used to premature ejaculation. Besides lovemaking for me was like self- abusing. Anyway, the next few days I felt very happy. I thought my prayers were accepted and I was given a very nice woman, not so sexy as Sara and very obedient! On the first day of April, we went to The Capital to apply for her passport. We went to The Capital by train with my wife's mother, sisters and her brother who was only one year younger than my wife was. The compartment had six seats and as the train travelled during the night, after an hour or two I said it was the right time to sleep. I asked my wife to come and sleep next to me on the top rack. It was a narrow rack suited only for one person but I held her tight in my arms and we slept next to each other until morning. After a while, I made love to her very quietly. I guess her mother noticed I was having sex with her daughter from the way I was breathing and keeping very quiet. My wife didn't object nor she did respond; she just laid down still. We then fell fast asleep. I think her mother was glad that after hearing so many rumors of my first marriage breakdown she had noticed that I had manhood as they used to say! I think it was on the 20th of April that we left The Capital. We didn't stay in London at all and went to Liverpool straight away. I had reserved a hotel apartment (called service flat) and we asked the taxi to take us there. We stayed in this service flat for one month. We started looking for a house or a furnished apartment to rent. Finally, we found a nice house fully furnished in a posh area of Liverpool to rent. The rent was 80 pounds per month. The owner was an architect working in Emirates and we had to pay the rent each month to his neighbor.

For ten days I didn't go to the University. I only informed my supervisor that I had returned. We used to sleep till late in the morning, and then used to go to The Big City center having lunch and returning to the hotel. In the evenings she was saying she was bored and we didn't know what to do. She could not speak English nor did she understand television programs. So I took her to the Village I was living before and introduced her to my friends. All my friends were surprised to see how young and beautiful my wife was. By the way, my car was with a garage. Just a few days before my departure to my country I had an accident. This time a woman driver ran into my car from behind on a rainy day. I had to leave my car with a garage. As the insurance had to pay for the repairs (changing the rear boot and painting it) they said it would take a month. I agreed and in fact appreciated it because I was going home and didn't know where to leave my car for one month. They charged me an extra ten pounds for keeping the car for an extra ten days.

Regarding our bedtime relations, we had two or sometimes three times a day sex relation together. Usually one when we slept, another one in early morning and one in the afternoon. She was the same every time, laid down without showing any enthusiasm just letting me do what I wanted to do. During daytime, she never let me take her clothes off. She never moaned or showed excitement; however, she never blamed me for premature ejaculation. Later she said she thought all men were like that; their sex relation lasted only for a few minutes, but some years later when she had heard from her friends their sex relations; especially some who had boasted and said their husbands made love to them for at least half an hour, she started groaning and blaming me not being able to give her pleasure. While in the hotel apartment, a friend of mine brought a rice cooker for us and showed her how to cook rice with lentil! My wife didn't know cooking at all. She even did not know how to make tea or fry eggs. After two weeks since we had come to Liverpool, my wife started groaning every evening, she said she was home sick and could not tolerate being lonely all day long. I had decided not to go to casinos and not to bet on horses, I took her to cinemas once or twice but she did not appreciate it because she could not understand English, she could only follow the sceneries. In addition, some films were either too sexy for her age or horror films. Once we went to see the film called Jaws, which was a horror film but had won many prizes. When we went to the cinema, there was a long queue and when the film started, the cinema was full of audience. Just five minutes of the film was shown that my wife screamed when seeing a shark attacked a young man and cut his legs off. The cinema attendant hurried towards us and told us to leave the cinema. In fact she was seventeen then and the film was for over eighteen years of age. I asked my wife to calm down and said the shark you saw was made of plastic; it was a robot but she said she could not tolerate seeing the shocking sceneries.

First time she received a letter from her parents she cried while reading it; especially when she read the letter of her eight-year-old sister. She cried a lot and said she missed all her family and told me she wanted to go back home. To calm her down I took her to the Play Boy Club, which was a posh casino. I had a small bet and surprisingly I won five pounds. I stopped betting, had a meal there, which was much cheaper than outside restaurants and returned home about midnight. The club was in The Big City center quite far from us. At least half an hour ride from our home. Therefore, we killed the time by amusing ourselves in the club. Anyway, taking her to the casino was the only way to calm her down and stop her from groaning and blaming me. We used to go to the Play Boy Club at least four times a week; sometimes with my friends. One night my wife and I were playing roulettes on a table when I noticed two young boys were talking about us. One of them was saying what a nice young girl this ugly man has with him and wished they could get her out of my hands! As they were whispering in our language, I could understand their dirty talks and dirty thinking. Therefore, we moved to another table and soon left the casino. On the way home, my wife said she had heard them as well and thanked me for leaving the casino. Our going to Playboy continued until she gave birth to her child. I remember going to the casino in January 1977 with her wearing pregnancy dress with her belly showing she was eight months pregnant! It was in May that she vomited and showed some signs of pregnancy. I took her to the University clinic and she gave a blood test for pregnancy. Two days later when I went to the clinic to get the results, the nurse told me she was sorry to inform me that the test was positive. I told her I was very glad to hear that. We soon wrote a letter to her parents and informed them she was pregnant!

It was in June that we could phone from our home directly to my country. One afternoon when I was at work in the university, her uncle had phoned from The Capital and talked to her. She was very glad to hear her uncle's voice and apparently had cried on the phone saying she was too lonely. This was conveyed to her parents and in their next letter; they said her mother and brother would come to see us in August. I was very happy to hear that and in a week's time we were able to phone them from our home in Liverpool, while this was not possible before that.

When I heard she was pregnant, I took her to a suburb clinic, which was quite near us. We visited a gynecologist who was very kind and welcomed us warmly. After filling a questionnaire he said she would deliver her baby on the 9th of February 1977. His prediction was correct. The doctor advised us what to do and what not to do. He told me that my wife was a baby and I should have been more careful not making her pregnant at that age. She was only seventeen when she had become pregnant. In a visit to my supervisor, he also said you have married with a baby, how could you? In fact, his daughter was also seventeen years old too. We used to visit the gynecologist in the clinic every fortnight and gradually I noticed her belly was growing. When she was six month pregnant, her belly had swallowed and I remember her with a perfectly round belly. Our time in Liverpool was passing by very happily. I gradually reduced my bedtime relation with her. Sometimes I made love to her while she was fast asleep. I had noticed that when she was asleep, she wouldn't wake up easily. Even if I played with her breasts or buttocks, she wouldn't wake up. So, gradually, I noticed that even making love to her while asleep she wouldn't wake up. This was like self- abusing only difference was in self- abusing everything was virtual dream but here it was half-virtual and half-real! Gradually as her stomach grew bigger, I did not make love to her heterosexually, I thought during last months of her pregnancy I shouldn't make love to her at all; instead I had found my way of satisfying myself. I abused myself more or less every night by making love to her when she was fast asleep. In such cases, if she woke, I pretended I was asleep and probably had a wet dream! This way of love making gradually became a habit for me. It was easy and as I was doing a wrong thing and always afraid of waking her up it was much more enjoyable than ordinary self- abusing. She also thought that heterosexual love making was wrong doing while she was pregnant, so she never blamed me for not demanding sex from her. Besides she was rather cold regarding sex, never showed any sign of enjoyment. She told me later that she thought it was the duty of a wife to lie down and let her husband to relieve himself. Maybe she was told that way, but later as she met lots of married couples and naturally talked about their sex relations or bed time experiences her sexual knowledge increased. In one of her meetings with a friend she was asked if we had sex relation every night. Her response was negative because she was pregnant, she said, her husband was considerate. I think she probably had noticed that she was wetted while she was asleep especially in early mornings, but she presumed I had a wet dream. She trusted in me and believed whatever I said at least for the first few years of our marriage.

In August, her mother and brother came to visit us. We went to London to fetch them from the airport. They stayed with us for one month. I took them to shopping centers and many sightseeing. My income had increased. We spent quite a lot of money for our leisure time; inviting friends to our house, going to casino most nights and phoning home a lot making our telephone bill very much. For the last two months of our stay in Liverpool we paid over two hundred pounds for the telephone bill. Our neighbor told us the bill of all the houses in that road (about 20 houses) did not sum up to that amount! A nice story was that my friend who was seven years older than me and had asked his parents to let him get married; told us he had decided to get married with a girl who was coming from my country to London to study language. We went to London with him to meet his fiancé. She was a nice young girl about 27 years old (ten years older than my wife) who had a B.Sc. degree had come to London to read for M.Sc. degree. She was a sophisticated girl, her accent was nice. She was taller than my wife. I did not know why she was not married yet; apparently she had known my friend for some years but my friend was not serious getting married with her. He used to say he had come across with quite a few number of girls from well-off and educated families but was not able to decide which one to choose. Now he was tempted to get married with his fiancé. My wife told him to make formal proposal to her. He did so and his fiancé asked her mother to come over to London for their wedding. I think it was late October when we were told everything was ready for their marriage. My wife told my friend that he must buy a wedding dress for her and give a small party. He got angry and said he wouldn't buy a wedding dress for her and does not believe in spending money for wedding ceremony. He had communist way of thinking. He was a high school teacher in The Capital who had saved some money in his career and apparently had immigrated to England for good. My wife phoned his fiancé and told her to get ready for marriage. We went to London on a Saturday morning. We went to our Embassy and made an appointment for a formal wedding. A registrar who was a Mullah invited us to his office for two o'clock in the afternoon. My wife, his fiancé, her mother and I attended the ceremony with groom. The Mullah first asked the bride if she would agree with the marriage. She said she demanded two hundred gold coins for getting married (That's the dowry). My friend got angry, he said he did not agree with that and intended to leave the room. My wife asked him not to ruin the arrangement and told her mother to advise her daughter. Mullah said minimum is fourteen gold coins and finally he accepted for this settlement. After the wedding, we left the office but the groom was upset with his wife for not telling him of her decision before going to the registration office. She pretended she was teasing him and she was not serious; if she was serious she would not have agreed with that settlement she said. In the evening, he took us to a posh restaurant in Kensington Street. There was an Arabic dancer to amuse the guests. It was rather nice but my friend seemed to be still angry at his fiancé. My wife tried to change the atmosphere and said many jokes. Later, we invited the newlywed couple to our house but we noticed that they always argued with each other on simple matters. Maybe it was their way of life!

During my wife's pregnancy, I did not have any sex relation with her of any kind. One afternoon when I was in The Big City center, I fancied going to the massage room I used to go before marriage. I told myself I would not have intercourse with the masseur only enjoy myself playing with her body. I convinced myself I should remain faithful to my wife but as I could not have sex relation with her, I would only play around with the masseur. I got into the massage room and asked the girl just to massage me. However, when she massaged my back I got very excited. When turned around, she asked me if I wanted any special treatment, then she said she would charge two pounds for oral and five pounds for full sex. I agreed with oral and soon she got on with it. I enjoyed it very much specially that my wife never allowed for oral sex. I decided to go and see this masseur at least once a week. Thereafter I went to this massage room at least once a week, on Tuesday afternoons I remember. After a month or two when I went to the massage room, a new masseur was employed. This girl was quite sexy and when I said I just want oral sex laughed at me and said why. I said because I was married and I didn't want to be unfaithful to my wife. She teased me and said how fool I was. She said if you don't want to be unfaithful you shouldn't come to places like this at all. She changed my mind by arguing and as she played around with me and tried to overwhelm me, I gave off and had full sex with her. I paid her five pounds and left the massage room happily. At home my wife said you look very happy today, I told her my work was finishing soon and I had obtained new results! So, going to the massage room and sometimes masturbating returned me to my old habits. To me self- abusing and meeting prostitutes was much more enjoyable than having sex with my wife or as it is said more fun than heterosexual relationship.

A month before the birth of our child, we received a letter from my wife's parents that they wanted to come to see my wife in her childbirth. On fourth day of February 1977, my mother-in-law and father-in-law arrived in London Heathrow airport. Before going to London, we went to see her physician. He said it was near her childbirth and she better not travel. However, she wanted to come to the airport and welcome her parents on their arrival. We set off from Liverpool early in the morning. We stopped in a motel to refresh and to fuel the car. She said she felt some pain in her stomach and back. This pain, which was a sign of giving birth, had started but we did not take it serious. Her parents arrived in Heathrow airport about two o'clock in the afternoon. I kissed her mother and also her father, but her father stood still and didn't appreciate me kissing him in front of others. Later, my wife said that her father had never kissed his own children, never mind you. However, my father used to kiss her daughters and daughter-in-laws in special occasions. We set off for Liverpool straightaway. I had put their luggage on the luggage rack I had installed on the car. My wife and her mother sat in the rear seats and I and her father were in font. We got to our home about six p m. The women prepared tea and then started unpacking their suitcases. They had brought some souvenirs for us which were mostly sweets and nuts. On Sunday we got up late and I took around my father-in-law to buy cigarettes. I noticed he was so pale that I thought he was ill. I asked him if there was anything wrong with him and he said no, no, I am feeling fine! Later, I was told that he was an opium addict and to give up his habit he had decided to come to stay with us for a month. In fact, as there was no opium in Liverpool or at least we did not know about it and as he did not want his son-in-law know about it, he had not brought opium with him from home either? For the first week of their stay, he was very unhappy I think but later he recovered soon. He never smoked opium afterwards and always said that it was because of the birth of his granddaughter that he had achieved giving up his habit. On Monday, I took my in-laws to The Big City center and we went to a famous store in Liverpool. My mother-in-law enjoyed herself very much shopping. I spent most of my time with my father-in-law and we had lunch outside. On Tuesday, we were invited by one of my colleagues who had come to Liverpool for study leave. He had come here with his family. He had three daughters and one son. They had come to Liverpool in September and we had gone to their house quite often. They were very kind and a pleasant family. All of them respected us and I used to play backgammon with my colleague. When they heard my in-laws were coming they invited us to go to their house as soon as we could. In fact we accepted their invitation gladly. On Tuesday we went to city center and looked around shops for quite a while. About four p.m. my wife said she felt a strong pain in her back. Later her face was full red and she sat down for a while. We rushed home, serious pain before giving birth had started! Her mother insisted she could wait for another day and we should not miss my colleague's invitation. We left for his house at about six p.m. and as soon as we got there, they were preparing supper for us. About ten o'clock my wife was blushed from pain and we decided to get her to the nearby hospital. It was about half an hour away. When we got there, a nurse examined my wife and told us her delivery time was reached. She said either cesarean or delivery by partial consciousness we can choose; we had decided for partial consciousness with her doctor and so the nurse gave her an injection and told me to leave the hospital until midday of next day. We went home and on the next day 9th of February I went to the hospital with my mother-in-law, but she was not allowed to be at her side, so I returned her back home and went to the hospital on my own. About two o'clock in the afternoon the nurse gave her another injection and told me to stay beside her till she delivers her baby. It took a long time before she was taken to the delivery room. The doctor said the baby's head hasn't turned downwards and they must use forceps to deliver the baby. I was standing on her bedside towards her head and was praying for her. Doctor asked my wife if she wanted a boy but she said she aimed for a girl. When the baby was delivered the doctor said it is a girl and my wife thanked God for that. The doctor said it is the first time I see a mother to be so glad for delivering a baby girl. It was ten o'clock in the evening that her baby was delivered. They had used forceps and so her head looked like a cucumber. They said they must keep the baby in incubator for at least three days. My wife was taken to a common room where some other women had just delivered their babies and so I went home. On Thursday afternoon about two o'clock in the afternoon, I and my in-laws went to the hospital to visit my wife. I was so glad that I had become a father and was feeling very proud about it. My daughter was inside a room for special care with some other children. I and my in-laws looked at her through the glass windows. She was rather dark and had black hair while other babies were white, either didn't have any hair on their head or had thin blonde hair. We noticed that other people looking behind the window were saying how beautiful this child was and some immediately said that this child must be colored! My mother-in-law was allowed for a short time to see her daughter. She then said I have come here to look after my daughter and forced me to ask her doctor to allow her to go home and rest at home sooner. Apparently they wanted to keep her in hospital for ten days. They wanted to teach her how to feed her baby child and how to clean her and look after her. As my in-law persisted, she was released on Sunday afternoon. We went to the hospital and fetched my wife and the new born baby wrapped in heavy blankets home. My wife was quite weak and really needed special care. She was recovering quickly and on Tuesday she got up from bed and did some of housekeeping herself. A nurse visited us regularly for two weeks until she was quite well. On Friday afternoon we went for shopping and left my wife at home alone with her baby. Her uncle's wife had ring from The Capital and were surprised to hear that she was left alone in the house.

On first of March, just a few days before they returned to my country, we went to London. My car was full and we carried my daughter in a cot with us. My daughter was not one month old that had her first trip outside her birthplace. In London, I took my in-laws to few sightseeing places and I remember my father-in-law liked the Madame Tussauds museum very much. When we were sitting in the planetarium, we had our baby's cot with us. After some time when the hall was in complete darkness and everybody was quiet listening to the commentary and watching the dome, suddenly our baby woke up and started crying. The guards run towards us and told us to leave the planetarium immediately. We all left the hall while I was very interested to watch what they had to say about astronomy. Outside the hall, we were told that children under five years were not allowed to the planetarium. We then walked around and my wife thought one of these guards was a statute. After my in-laws left London for home we returned to Liverpool. In the next few months we looked after our daughter very carefully. It had made our life very warm and we were very enthusiastic of having such a pleasant event.

In few months after my daughter was born, I did not have much sex relation with my wife as I remember. I do not know why, perhaps because I did not insist nor she did show any desire to have sex. Three months gone, she said she wanted to go home and visit her family. I did not resist and in fact, I wanted her to go home for a while. I thought when she goes home I can watch whatever TV channels I want, spend as much time as I could in the casino (we couldn't go to casino with our child or leave her alone at home) and most of all I could go to massage rooms and enjoy myself with prostitutes. I told my wife that I hoped when she goes home I could work harder and get my thesis finished by the time she returns. Meanwhile my father said in his letter that the land I had bought in The Big City near my hometown had gained a good price rise and advised me it is better I sell it. I would get 20 times the price I had bought it. I responded if I sell this I had to buy a piece of land somewhere else. Now, I wish I had listened to his advice and sold it. Even if I had gone home with my wife and sold it, I would have gained a lot of money or I could have bought a small house somewhere. How stupid I was!

Anyway, in June 1977 my wife went home for a one-month visit. I took her to London Heathrow airport and on return; I was speeding with my little car. In one occasion, I skipped an accident and from then on I decided to slow down. I wanted to get home as soon as possible. I got home in the evening. I had a short rest and then set off for Playboy casino. I spent about fifty pounds. It was a heavy loss. I remember I got very nervous, I tried all kinds of tricks to get my money back, but it was not my night. The next day I got up late. I had decided to go to a massage room. I had masturbated in early morning but in the afternoon I decided to go and discover a new massage room. I remember I found a new massage room from an advertisement in local newspaper. I soon found the place and knocked the door. There was a young woman about 25 years old with a nice figure. I started foreplay but I was not much excited. While kissing her, I remembered my wife and told myself my wife was much nicer than her and I blamed myself for doing wrong thing. I paid the girl and left her rather disappointed. On the way back home I decided not to visit any massage rooms and keep myself for my wife. But this decision did not last long as usual. Only three or four days I stayed at home and watched Television. I remember the year 1977 was called silver wedding; that is it was 25th anniversary of Queen Elizabeth's rule. Television had a special program called "Royal Heritage" and I liked watching it. In addition, I used to follow racing on Television. I had decided to concentrate on writing my thesis seriously, but after a week, I forgot all about it. I tried different massage rooms.

I had bought a cam recorder and a projector. The films we shot were taken on 8 mm films and were processed by the company of the filmmakers; Kodak and Agfa were two famous brands I used to buy. The cam recorder and the projector had cost me about four hundred pounds. It usually took about ten days to get the film processed. Even then film duration was only three minutes. When my daughter was born we bought this home movie set and took several films from her. In the first six months, we filled at least two photo albums and a handful of films. After a couple of weeks, I received a call from my wife saying she missed me but her parents insisted to allow her to stay for two months and I agreed. In the two months that she was away, I tried to enjoy myself as much as I could. After a month, watching television was getting boring for me. I could not concentrate much on writing my thesis either. The weather was very nice and I wanted to chase street girls once again. I had bought some porno films and used to spend some time watching them. Some of the films had a very nice and exciting story behind them and watching them always ended up with self- abusing. Even then, I fancied looking for new massage rooms or street girls and I was successful. At least once a week I had a new experience. Before embarking to go ahead with a new experience, I was very excited and nothing could stop me from my decision, but just after having relieved myself, I was very depressed and always decided not to do it again. I told myself I am married, I have a young wife and I must be faithful to her. On the other hand having sex with just one woman, no matter a street girl or my wife, became gradually boring. I always wanted someone new; perhaps it had become a habit. Of course, self-abusing was another bad habit. I continued buying porno magazines and porno films. I continued imagining strange porno sceneries in bed and at last every other day I abused myself. This was the main reason why I never had a successful heterosexual relationship with anybody, my wife or street girls. Of course, street girl's main aim was to earn money in the shortest possible time and they were always satisfied with a client like me who paid them readily and finished his job in shortest possible time.

After two months, my wife returned to England and I drove to London Heathrow airport and fetched her back home. Only two days before her return I had visited a massage room. When we arrived in our home, we were rather tired of the trip and slept early. Next day, it was Sunday and got up rather late. We made love after so many months, perhaps after one year. It was the first time she showed she wanted sex and when I had premature orgasm I could see from her eyes that she was not satisfied. I blamed myself for what I had done in the past two months and was sorry for myself. I told her I will try it in half an hour or so but even then I was not able to satisfy her and I could feel how much she got depressed although she did not tell me anything nor did she blame me for it. I always regretted for what I had done to myself. I thought I had abused myself and it made me depressed temporarily. This had become a habit for me and I could not give it up. Now that my wife had returned, we could have heterosexual relationship but both were not very keen on it. She was young, shy, and expected foreplay and some kind of treatment to get ready. I had used to quick action. When I got the urge for sex, I wanted to have it done as soon as possible. I could not prolong my desire and keep myself for more than a minute or two!

She used to tell me that I was not handsome and it was always her wish to have a handsome husband. Once I asked her if she knew I was married before and she said she did know about it. She asked about Sara and I told her that although I loved her very much but due to some unexpected events we had to get divorced. I also told her about my first love, Lidia and more or less told her what had happened between us. I asked her if she loved any one while in school and she confessed that she had a boyfriend. She asked me if I could guess who he was and my guesses were wrong. In fact, later she said her boyfriend was the son of one of their neighbors and was very handsome. She said her mother was against their marriage. My wife always says that her marriage with me was a forced marriage and her mother had made all the arrangements. She still curses her mother and believes she was jealous about her and did not want her happiness.

In the second year of our marriage, we spent a lot of attention on our daughter. Both of us loved her very much. I used to say that this is the most beautiful child in the world! On the first anniversary of birthday of my daughter we were invited by a colleague to Leeds. The birthday of one of their daughters coincided with my daughter. I was wearing a new suit and my wife and my daughter had their best clothes on. It was a memorable ceremony and they made a nice movie from the party. In February 1978, I received a letter from home that my mother, my second sister and her two-year-old son were coming to visit us in England. My father's business was flourishing and he had become quite rich. They arrived on the fifteenth of February and I fetched my family from the airport and took them to Liverpool by my car. I am surprised now that although my car was a small car, how many people I drove with it. They stayed with us for one month and did plenty of shopping. In fact my mother had come to have a medical checkup and mainly to buy wedding dress for my brother's fiancé who was my wife's cousin. She was a very beautiful and cute girl only one year younger than my wife and one year younger than my brother was. In fact, my wife was very glad to hear that her beloved cousin was going to be her sister-in-law as well. My mother bought very expensive clothes for her and some clothing's for my wife, my daughter and me as well. She asked my father to send her more money and he sent fifteen thousand pounds for me to give her. I did not take any of that but we spent a lot of money. Her checkup cost two hundred and fifty pounds. She also bought hearing aid for six hundred pounds. I also received a letter from my father that he could send me money in case I wanted to buy a house in Liverpool. I told our neighbor about it, he said the property owner intends to sell his house. He said it would cost only eleven thousands pounds. I told my wife that we intend to go home and stay in my country for good, so there is no point buying a house in Liverpool. How fool I was. I could have bought the house, let it for rent, and saved the rent money as an income. My mother left us after a month with a lot of luggage.

On first of March 1978, we were hearing some news from my country regarding humanitarian discomfort in my country. Actually, it was about a year that the main talk of my countrymen was about politics and it had become a sign of intellectuality to talk about politics and everybody seemed to have a handful of advice for the regime! A friend of us who came from my country just a week before told us some two thousand persons had been killed in demonstrations! It was a big exaggeration. I used to look at newspapers every day to read the latest news about my country. I remember I saw in Guardian that only two people were killed in demonstrations of first of April in my hometown. My wife was embarrassed very much and insisted we must go home as soon as we could. She was getting worried about her family, but now I guess she was probably more worried about her boyfriend who was a political activist and had been in prison for a year or two. She told me this many years later. On the other hand my supervisor told me I should finish my studies and urged me to hand him the final draft. In fact, I had given my writings to his secretary to type it on stencils. I handed him the final copy in May and he set the date for my exam in early June. During this time we were getting ready to go home. We bought three big cases and some suitcases for packing our staffs. I received a letter from my father that if I want to take a car with me to my country he would send me money to buy a Mercedes, but

I denied his offer and said I would rather buy a Datsun when I get back home.

I attended the oral exam just on time (about 1 p.m.). After the presentation, my supervised congratulated me for my graduation. My wife was expecting me and our neighbor welcomed me and told us we must celebrate. We had prepared a cake and invited them inside and took some photographs for this occasion. Our neighbor said she would look after our daughter in the evening and told us we must have a big celebration and enjoy ourselves. We went to the Playboy casino in the evening and had a good meal there and played Roulette for the last time. On the way home, we called on our neighbor but my daughter was asleep and we left her there until 9 o'clock in the following morning.

Just after graduation, we started packing our luggage. I booked air tickets for 16th of June. We also put an advert in local newspaper for the sale of our car. Two days before our departure a man came to see the car and to buy it for his daughter. Apparently, she had just passed her driving license test and was very keen to buy the car. I sold it for 850 pounds. I gave fifty pounds discount and asked the buyer to pay me cash. I also asked them to come and collect the car a day before our departure. He accepted it and came on Friday evening to take the car. When he took the car and drove away from us, my wife and I had tears in our eyes because we missed it very much. We had plenty of good memories with it, it had become a part of our life. No other cars in our life brought such emotions for us and I still miss that small car. We sent some of our luggage (three big trunks and several boxes full of books) by airfreight and took only few cases with ourselves. Our neighbor took us to the airport. We flew to London, changed the flight terminal, and flew home.

My stay back home and the events that lead to divorce my beloved wife is another story, which I will explain it in detail in the next volume of my book.

Printed in the United States
By Bookmasters